**JOHN
LENNON**

**ONE
DAY AT
A TIME**

JOHN LENNON

ONE DAY AT A TIME

A PERSONAL BIOGRAPHY OF THE SEVENTIES

BY ANTHONY FAWCETT

GROVE PRESS, INC., NEW YORK

Acknowledgments

This page is to thank the following people, with love and appreciation for feeling the conceptual energy of this book and for making it possible:

Mario Amaya, New York; Fabio Barraclough, Rugby; Franz Birrer, Los Alamitos; Margrit and Andy Chandler and family, Huntington Harbor; Colin Clark, London; Paul Denis, Brussels; Henry Diltz, Los Angeles; Chip Douglas, Los Angeles; Al and Jean, Entella Hotel, San Francisco; Tom Fairhead, Art Department, Abingdon School; Judith Fawcett-Ryley, Ramsgate; Les Fawcett, Hillingdon Heath; Heinrich Grieder, Schauffhausen; Sharon Inahara, San Francisco; John Kosh, Los Angeles; Bob LeShufy, New York; Mackays of Chatham; Professor Roberta Markman, Cal State, Long Beach; Claudia Menza, Grove Press, New York; Judy Moll, Los Angeles; Karen Mullarkey, Picture Editor, Rolling Stone; Ed Newman, Paris; Frances Schoenberger, Hollywood; Linda Stearns, New English Library, London; Abner Stein, London; Bob Tanner, New English Library, London; Gayle Theisen, Washington, D.C.; Ritchie Yorke, Toronto.

Finally, a special thank you to: Francis Greenburger and Laura Torbet; Fred Jordan, my editor at Grove Press; Ken Deardoff, master-designer, who has added a new dimension to my words; Christina Birrer, who shared with me in the conception and realization of this book; Lawrence Durrell, Henry Miller and Anaïs Nin, for giving me the desire to write; and John and Yoko Lennon for the chance to be involved in their heraldic journey.

CONTENTS

This book is dedicated to Chrissy

INTRO- DUCTION

Man Ray, the Dadaist painter and photographer, once said to me: "The artist is the only true sage. He comes to us with open mind and with open hands. When his work confronts others he is not up for trial, it is the spectator, if anyone, who is putting himself on record. Time has proven this again and again . . . The streets are full of admirable craftsmen, but so few practical dreamers."

This book is about the growth of the artist John Lennon, a poet, a primitive musician, and certainly a practical dreamer. John, as a mirror of our times, has always innately felt the need to change, to search for new ideas, new experiences, new people. The idea of "one day at a time" works for John, as it does for many of us, not only to keep his own life and work in perspective but also to cope with the paraphernalia and visual jetsam which constantly assault our senses. John is constantly telling us, "This is where I am at this moment, this is what's going on."

"We only know a small part of what really happened to John in the years since he met Yoko Ono in 1966 at the Indica Gallery in London," the American writer Pete Hamill has written. "The details belong to John Lennon alone." It was during this period that I became involved in John's life, when I was working in London as an art critic, and at first I was involved only with ideas and projects for art events: the Acorn Event, which was a conceptual sculpture John and Yoko presented at a National Sculpture Exhibition that I helped to organize, and John's Erotic Lithographs, a project I instigated with an American publisher. Then early in 1969 I gave up my art criticism to work with John and Yoko full time, running their office, organizing their daily schedules, cataloging their writings and films.

The job quickly became a twenty-four hour day and night involvement and soon my life was totally meshed with theirs. It was an exciting and exhilarating experience but it was also hard and demanding. John and Yoko began to depend on me, and expected me to supply them with any

detail of their myriad projects—past, present or future. Every intricacy of their life was channeled through me. When their problems and traumas became too pressing they became recluses in their own home and would not see or talk to anyone; I became their only contact with the outside world.

Many of us have fallen under the spell of John Lennon, who has the ability to inspire and to mesmerize people. Indeed, he inspired Paul McCartney, George Harrison and Ringo Starr and what they did is already history. I think Pete Hamill summed up John's legacy brilliantly when he wrote in *Rolling Stone:*

''The twenty Beatles albums are there; the voices are forever young. John Lennon, the young man with the guitar who went to Hamburg and played the eight hour gigs with the others, popping pills to stay up, drawing on some tough maniac energy. 'You see,' he explained later, 'we wanted to be bigger than Elvis . . .'

''Bigger than Elvis. Bigger than Sinatra. Bigger than God. John told everybody how the Beatles were more popular than Jesus Christ and for a couple of weeks that summer most of the Western world seemed to go into an uproar. Was the world really that innocent so short a time ago? No. It was just that John Lennon was explaining that the world had changed and the newspapers had to catch up; we were not going to have any more aw-shucks heroes. So we could all run in the endless emptiness of the rugby field in *A Hard Day's Night,* rising or falling, in slow motion or fast, but sooner or later we would have to grow up. The Beatles were custodians of childhood. They could not last.

''And yet . . . and yet, it seemed when it was finally over, when they had all gone their separate ways, when Brian Epstein lay dead and Apple was some terrible mess and the lawyers and the agents and the money men had come in to paw the remains, it often seemed that John was the only one whose heart was truly broken . . . From some corner of his broken heart, John gave the most bitter interviews, full of hurt and resentment, covered over with the language of violence. In some way, he had been the engine of the group, the artistic armature driving the machine beyond its own limits, restless, easily bored, in love with speed the way Picasso was in love with speed, and possessed of a hoodlum's fanatic heart . . .

''John moved through everything else: Bed-Ins, peace posters, a phony drug arrest, the acorns planted in the plastic pots in the Coventry Cathedral. He followed Yoko into the rare air of the avant-garde, banging up against Cage and Bartok, undergoing a rebarbarization of his music as if running to some older, purer vision he had of himself, created in the loneliness of the Liverpool art school when he was convinced he was a genius. Bagism, Shagism, Rubin and Hoffman, acid and anger; the marriage in Gibraltar, seventeen stitches in a car crash in Scotland, the M.B.E. handed back to the Queen, the Plastic Ono Band, his hair long, his hair short, the neat, precise features wearing a series of masks, his life with Yoko a series of public events. Working Class Hero. Some Time in New York City. Power to the People. And even deeper into America: into its crazed, filthy Nixonian heart and the immigration case, and that form of the Higher Paranoia that comes because you are a victim in a time when all the other victims have proof and you have none.

" 'All we are saying . . .' It was a long way from Chuck Berry . . ."

I shared intimately in days when it was magic to be around John and days when it was torture. For the most part his life was filtered through pain. The Beatles were breaking up and John and Yoko's own relationship was on the brink of collapse. My last few months with them were turbulent; more and more I found myself in the cross fire of their disintegrating life. I stayed with them until they left to have Primal Therapy in California, in May 1970.

For John this was an important and crucial period of his life—a time of intense growth. The events of these two years, from 1968 to 1970, radically changed the course of his development. In the book I have followed his journey through the seventies to the happy conclusion of his immigration problems—and the birth of John and Yoko's son, Sean Ono Lennon. I see these events as the beginning of a new phase of great productivity in John's career.

Lennon is an exciting, creative human being, and it is his deeper, underlying energies which interest me. In this book I have tried to understand the man, the artist, and his inner workings. If such an understanding is in some way communicated to the reader I will be satisfied. Henry Miller wrote: "I don't care who the artist is, if you study him deeply, sincerely, detachedly, you will find that he and his work are one." So it is with John Lennon.

Anthony Fawcett.
New York City, May 1976.

PART ONE

THE MAN

ONE DAY AT A TIME

My life changed the day that I met John Lennon. He was sitting on the stairs of the Arts Laboratory in Drury Lane, barely recognizable under a cloth cap pulled down over the familiar round specs, and I think I would have missed him had it not been for the unmistakable presence of Yoko huddling next to him. I had met her briefly several times before at various galleries, and had once written about her work, so I stopped to talk. It was spring 1968, the occasion of their first exhibition together, but John seemed totally aloof from the event. He looked as though he hadn't slept for days, his stubbly face markedly thinner than the chubby visage of earlier Beatle days. He was shabbily dressed in a worn-out Edwardian-style suit and moved around restlessly, chain smoking Gauloises cigarettes. His piercing eyes seemed to size me up as Yoko talked about the show and introduced me to a friend—Hugh Shaw, a quiet but important exhibitions coordinator from the Arts Council. After a while I left to mingle with the crowd which seemed intent on destroying the wooden sculptures that had been designed as "objects to be taken apart or added to." As the opening drew to a close I was taken aback when John came over and asked me if I'd like to join him and Yoko and Hugh Shaw for dinner. It was raining and we ran down the street to a nearby Tandouri restaurant, went in, and took a corner table way in the back.

Without even a glance at the exotic Indian menu, John ordered fish and chips, which he proceeded to smother in tomato ketchup. He was obviously tired but he also struck me as vulnerable; when he talked he talked fast, running sentences and subjects together in a verbal torrent hard to follow. Then he would be quiet, retreating completely from the conversation, seemingly lost within himself.

The talk turned to art, in particular Yoko's art. The man from the Arts Council listened attentively as she sparkled with exuberance at this chance to explain her films and events. As I had noticed at earlier events at the Indica Gallery, Yoko was a marvelous public relations woman when it came to persuading the right people to help carry out her ideas.

She might be standing quietly in the corner of a room looking frail enough for the wind to blow her down, and then her timid figure would be transformed suddenly into that of a dynamic conjurer of words and emotions, articulating verbal sparklers to a spellbound audience.

A crowd had gathered outside the restaurant on the narrow Soho pavement. While we sipped our coffee, John's chauffeur Les Antony circled the block in the white Rolls Royce, and when we got up to leave John offered me a ride home.

As we sped down the New Kings Road Yoko questioned me about the National Sculpture Exhibition which I was helping to organize; she was interested in which artists had been included in the show and what the criteria were for their selection. When the Rolls glided to a halt outside my terraced house in Parsons Green, John jumped out, asked to "bum a fag" and followed me inside. He stopped abruptly in the hall, shocked at seeing on the wall some large paintings by his art school friend Jonathan Hague. "Where d'er git those?" he asked incredulously, staring at the canvases. Hague had recently been given a prestigious one-man exhibition in a large private London art gallery, sponsored by "Lennon and McCartney." I had reviewed the show for several art magazines and had got to know him. All the paintings that hadn't been sold had been left at my house because he lived up in the north of England but wanted to keep his work in the big city.

Laughing at my explanation, John proceeded to run all over the house looking at the paintings. I went upstairs in search of cigarettes and tried to wake my housemate Simmonds. "John Lennon's downstairs!" I shouted. "Where are the fags?" In a daze he tried to sit up, just as John came bursting into the room. "That's a good'un," John said, looking at another painting, and muttered "'ello" to the pajamaed figure in the bed. Not quite believing this was really happening, my friend struggled to get out an audible answer, and as we left the room he slumped back under his covers.

Downstairs in the living room, Yoko whispered in John's ear for a minute and then asked me whether they could both contribute a sculpture to the exhibition I was working on. Pleased and excited by the idea, I agreed to talk to my associate Fabio Barraclough, the chief organizer and leading force behind the show. John screwed up his face and chuckled to himself; I think he was thoroughly entertained at the thought of being in an important art exhibition. He appeared enthusiastic and was certainly more cheerful than he had been at dinner. As we walked outside he asked me to keep in touch and let them have any news of a decision as soon as possible. Then he ducked into the back seat with Yoko close be-

Anthony Fawcett with John and Yoko at Gregg's basement macrobiotic restaurant in Notting Hill Gate, London, the first time he met them "completely on their own, out of the turmoil of offices and recording studios."

hind him. As I waved goodbye the white blur of the Rolls quickly disappeared into the cold London night, and I was left pondering this bizarre start of what was to become an enlightening and surreal relationship with John Lennon.

At the Abbey Road recording studios a gruff uniformed receptionist led me down a long narrow corridor with faded yellow walls that appeared more institutional than inspirational. But my feeling about the place changed when the two massive steel doors of Studio One were swung open. Almost stumbling over John, who was sitting on the floor, I found myself in a miniscule room, surrounded by all four Beatles. My immediate feelings were prismatic as I glanced around, momentarily taking in the faces which were as familiar as those of my own family, yet there was something unnerving about the experience, and I unconsciously held my breath. Paul was sitting at a grand piano laughing as he banged out chords, George, totally engrossed in his guitar, pivoted atop a high stool, and Ringo looked lost, hemmed in behind his drums and soundproof boarding. Yoko beckoned me to sit down next to her and John. As they started talking George Martin's voice boomed over the loudspeakers from the control room, requesting them all to listen to a playback, and John's words were drowned out by the music.

A month had gone by since my first evening with John and Yoko. Fabio Barraclough had been receptive to the idea of their contributing a sculpture to the exhibition and we had brought the matter up at the committee meetings. Although several of the older and more conservative members were opposed, Fabio had given the go-ahead, and I had relayed the news to Yoko. Several days later a cryptic message had summoned me to the recording studios.

At the end of the playback George Martin signaled from behind the thick glass observation window and everyone trooped into the control booth. The complex eight-track recording console dominated the room, which was a veritable labyrinth of electronic gadgets, tangled wires and gigantic speakers. John lit up a Disque Bleu, and joked with the engineer as he sat down behind the board. During the next playback he fiddled with every knob and lever, his face taut with concentration until Mal, the gentle giant of a roadie, brought in the tea tray and work stopped for a "cuppa."

John and Yoko came over to where I was standing, and we started to talk about the exhibition. I asked if they had decided what their sculpture was going to be, as this was the question everyone was curious about. Yoko whispered to John for a few moments, they laughed, and then John said:

"It's a secret—we can't tell you cos it'll spoil it." I hesitated, unsure of what to say, and then explained that I really had to know to get the final approval from the organizing committee of the exhibition. They whispered to each other again and finally Yoko said: "Well, it was John's idea and it is so beautiful that I copied it—our sculpture is going to be two acorns planted in the ground, one facing to the East, the other to the West. The acorns will symbolize our meeting and love for each other, and also the uniting and growth of our two cultures."

My immediate reaction was mixed. I tried to imagine how the acorns would fit into a survey of the best contemporary British sculpture—which at that time were mostly figurative stone and bronze pieces, or abstract "New Generation" brightly painted steel constructions. But the conceptual idea of acorns as "living art" was original and certainly something the Dadaists would have been proud of. Conceptual art as a movement was already starting to make an impact among the avant-garde galleries in Germany and Italy, and Yoko had been one of the first artists to put on a conceptual exhibition in London. I realized that what Yoko was doing for John was changing his attitude about art—and everything else—by showing him that anything was possible, and more importantly that all the ideas he had in his head should be brought out into the open and followed through, not just left as fantasies.

The other Beatles were now shouting at John to get back to work. I stayed to listen to a few more playbacks and when I left John reminded me to come into the Wigmore Street Apple offices the following week, to discuss the exhibition plans in more detail.

Over tea at Fortnum and Mason, Fabio was a little shocked by the conceptual sculpture idea, but he told me not to worry because he would clear it through the committee; he was doubtful, though, about including the Acorn piece in the official catalog. When I relayed this to John and Yoko a few days later at Apple headquarters, their reaction was "well, fuck it, we'll make our own catalog." "You can write the notes," John said, promptly showing me an empty office to use.

The whole place was swarming with people. The Beatles and their newly formed group of companies had taken over the entire fifth floor of an office block, while their Georgian mansion on Savile Row was being rebuilt and furnished. All the rooms in the Wigmore Street office led off a central reception area filled with reporters and photographers hoping to get an audience, assorted freaks and musicians, and a sprinkling of fans sitting it out for an autograph.

After completing some rough notes for the catalog I returned to the small office where John and Yoko were sitting at opposite sides of a desk, drinking coffee. Paul McCartney and Neil Aspinal were also in the room reading through proofs of the "authorized" Beatles biography, pages of which lay scattered all over the desk and floor. Before I had time to start a conversation, one of the *Daily Mirror*'s top show-biz reporters appeared in the doorway with his photographer. John and Paul, both apparently horrified at the unannounced intrusion, muttered in unison "get 'im out." "Just a quick photo, boys," he pleaded, while the photographer took aim and popped his flashbulb without waiting for an answer. "And what's all this big business you're getting into?" I was surprised when John shouted at him sarcastically, "Get out, we're not telling you anything!" Paul gave him an equally hard time but the reporter didn't seem unduly perturbed as he left the room with no story.

The next day I saw how the Beatle myth perpetuated itself. I had witnessed a total lack of cooperation from John and Paul, and yet larger than life in the *Daily Mirror* was a full page article on "The Big Business Beatles," complete with a rundown of Apple's staff and business ambitions.

The photograph for the front of the Acorn catalog was taken in the usual last minute manner. Yoko called me late in the evening from a basement macrobiotic restaurant, informed me that they were ready to have a photo taken, and asked if I could be there with a reliable photographer in half an hour. I agreed and immediately called Keith McMillan, with whom I had worked on art assignments. He met me at the restaurant in Notting Hill Gate and we found John and Yoko seated on cushions on the floor in one of the back rooms. They were both dressed from head to toe in white, and looked immaculate. There was a freshness, an effervescence about their appearance. John's chestnut hair was neatly parted as if in unison with Yoko, whose jet-black flowing locks cropped her small face with severity, accentuating the curves of her heavy eyebrows and penetrating coal eyes. An air of tranquility pervaded the room. This was the first time I had been with them completely on their own, out of the turmoil of offices and recording studios. In the stillness their faces radiated happiness, and I saw in their expressions and in the way they looked at each other a kind of inner peace. It was at that moment that I realized they were both very gentle, even fragile, beings.

John and Yoko wanted an unusual and special photograph, directly related to the idea of the event. Keith knew instinctively what to do. He had them crouch behind one end of the long narrow table and placed the two plastic pots containing the acorns at the other end, close to his camera.

I had witnessed a total lack of cooperation from John and Paul and yet larger than life in the *Daily Mirror* was a full-page article on "The Big Business Beatles," complete with a rundown of Apple's staff and business ambitions.

The unusual perspective in the resulting photo gave the impression of John and Yoko flowering out of the pots. It was simple and conceptual; John and Yoko were pleased.

The catalog was now complete and ready for the printers. Keith's photo was used full frame on the cover and the inside spread consisted of John and Yoko's statements about their sculpture. "This is what happens when two clouds meet," read John's; opposite it Yoko's read: "This is what happens when two clouds meet (the piece is John's idea but it was so good that I stole it)." On the back cover was a short commentary I had written, part of which read: "The thoughts behind it [the event] are beautiful and its true fulfillment through the cycle of growth is an end in itself—the best idea that can ever be conceived as a work of art—mother nature is supreme, overriding man's artificial constructions."

John was really playing Yoko's game now, and playing it well. They had been living together for barely two months and already John was totally absorbed by her ideas and lifestyle. The rarified air of the avant-garde appealed to him and was a welcome change from the problems of the Beatles; creatively John was bubbling with ideas for art pieces and events, equaling Yoko's own continuous stream of inspirations. It was hard to imagine that ten weeks earlier he had been at the Maharishi's mountain retreat in India, totally depressed and writing such desperate lyrics as "Yes, I'm lonely wanna die," and "Feel so suicidal even hate my rock and roll." Being with Yoko had certainly effected a sudden transformation within John.

As the opening date of the exhibition neared, John's plans for the Acorn Event became more elaborate. First he ordered a silver-plated plaque to be engraved with the names of the sculptures: " 'John' by Yoko Ono, 'Yoko' by John Lennon, Sometime in May 1968." Then he devised a practical extension to the work by finding a large circular wrought-iron garden seat to cover the spot where the acorns would be buried. He thought this would also be perfect for people who wanted to sit and contemplate the sculpture.

John and Yoko decided to drive up to Coventry Cathedral on the day of the preview [June 15, 1968] for an official ceremony to plant the acorns before the exhibition was open to the public. The main sculptures were to be shown inside the open-air ruins of the old Cathedral, which had been bombed during the war. Fabio was not sure where the Cathedral authorities would allow the acorns to be buried and even hinted that there might be trouble from one Canon Verney. Apparently the Canon was worried in case it appeared that the Cathedral was condoning the couple's "out-of-wedlock" relationship.

The Acorn Event in progress. Far left: A confrontation about where to plant the acorns—pictured left to
right, Fabio Barraclough, organizer of the National
Sculpture Exhibition; Yoko; John; Anthony Fawcett;
and Canon Verney of Coventry Cathedral. Center:
John digs the hole for his pot of acorns. Above:
John and Yoko sit on their completed sculpture—a
wrought-iron garden seat covering the buried
acorns.

On the big day I met with John and Yoko at Kenwood, John's country
house atop the St. Georges Hill estate in Surrey. It was surreal to see the
wrought-iron garden seat on a trailer hitched to the sleek white Rolls,
with its black windows and space age TV antenna protruding from the
roof. John and Yoko ran out of the house laughing and excited, both
dressed in white and carrying the pots of acorns. Les, the chauffeur, put a
couple of shovels in the trunk, checked to see if the garden seat was
firmly secured, and then we set off for Coventry, a three hour drive. During the trip we talked about the hypocrisy of the art world and related
subjects, but John was immersed in the gadgetry and electronic
paraphernalia that surrounded the back seat—tape recorders, a television and video cassette player, a telephone connected to the international exchange and a custom designed "floating" record player (which
played no matter how bumpy the road became).

On arrival the welcoming committee was nowhere to be found. John decided that we should get out and walk across the pedestrian mall to the
restaurant where the reception was to be held. Within a few seconds a
cry went out as John was recognized and a gang of kids rushed over to
stare, following us at a distance. By the time we approached the restaurant
the crowd had grown to alarming proportions and we were suddenly
surrounded by a mob shouting for autographs. Although Yoko appeared nervous and a little apprehensive, John seemed happy to oblige
and even pleased by the attention. He remained calm, handling the
situation with ease, but became politely firm when it was time to move on.

After drinks and introductions Fabio quickly escorted us to the exhibition
site at the Cathedral, where we were met by the lugubrious Canon
Verney. Despite a facade of polite exchanges the reality I had feared
now manifested itself. "Unfortunately," the Canon intoned (and I
knew at once what was to follow), "the Cathedral authorities have
decided they cannot permit you to put your work in the main exhibition
area, as it is on consecrated ground."

I thought Yoko was going to explode but before she could protest the
Canon had turned away, requesting us to join him in the Dean's office,
"where everything could be talked out in private." After the door closed
a heated discussion ensued, mainly between Yoko and the Canon, with
John throwing in a word here and there. While Verney tried in vain to
explain the Cathedral's position, Yoko became more and more worked
up. The last straw was his insisting that the acorns were not really
sculpture anyway. At this Yoko got hysterical and red in the face and
began to scream at the Canon, demanding that all the leading sculptors
in the country be immediately telephoned—she felt that they would de-

fend her ideas. He assented and an attempt was made to call several artists. Henry Moore's house was reached but he was out. After more arguing, during which John flopped into a chair bewildered, a compromise solution was finally agreed upon. John and Yoko would be given a special area to plant the acorns on a grass lawn near the new Cathedral. Several of the younger New Generation sculptors had set up their large constructions on the surrounding grounds, so the compromise was actually not at all demeaning; and anyway the main exhibition was covered with medieval stone slabs hardly suitable for burying acorns.

The activity shifted to the lawn in question, and the Acorn Event itself took place within a few minutes. Les appeared with the shovels, and after carefully working out which was East and which was West, John and Yoko started to dig holes for their respective pots of acorns. Fabio, the Canon (who was all smiles now), and a small group of fascinated spectators all looked on; Keith McMillan darted around taking photos. When the pots were in position and the earth filled in, everybody stood quietly as John spoke a few words about the event, expressing hope that the East and West would soon be united.

The ceremony over, John was anxious to leave. He appeared tense and shaken from the unexpected confrontation. After making arrangements for the exhibition stewards to distribute the Acorn catalog free of charge, hasty goodbyes were exchanged and we were soon on the freeway speeding back toward London, our anger reverberating around the car. John, who had kept his emotions to himself during the day, now ranted and raved, his swearing sharply accentuated by his nasal Liverpudlian accent.

The silver plaque engraved with the titles of acorn sculptures: "Yoko" by John Lennon, "John" by Yoko Ono, Some time in May 1968.

This was not, however, the end of the story. In what seemed like spiteful retaliation Canon Verney refused to allow John and Yoko's catalog to be distributed to the public. People might think, he claimed, that the exhibit had something to do with the artists' personal relationships, which he found distasteful. John, in an effort to alleviate his anger at this rebuff, sent a letter to the Canon thanking him for his Christian attitude. He said that Christ stood for people and would probably have loved him and Yoko for their contribution.

A week after the opening of the exhibition the acorns were dug up in the middle of the night and stolen. The police were called in; it made great news for the local papers. John and Yoko had to send a second set of acorns and we arranged for security guards to keep watch on the exhibit for the duration of the show.

The Acorn Event was important to John, not only because it was one of his first art projects with Yoko, but also because it was a gesture for peace—"the East and West coming together," a utopian theme which was to underlie much of his philosophy and music. The Acorn Event, as a conceptual peace statement, was the forerunner of the Bed-Ins and the "acorns-for-peace" which John and Yoko later sent to a number of world leaders. At that time, John stated: "Perhaps if they plant them and watch them grow they might get the idea into their heads."

THE BALLAD OF JOHN AND YOKO

"For the two years before I met Yoko I had got terribly depressed. My life just seemed to have no purpose whatsoever. I wrote songs out of despair. She taught me to think again, to understand what had been happening to me and therefore why it was ridiculous to go on as I was."   (John Lennon, 1969)

"When I met John I was at the point of disappearance, in the eyes of other people and myself. Where could I go after I'd done the silent music and they still didn't catch up on it? You see, the things that I did then I feel were in a field that no one has really touched on yet. I think I had something to offer but people did all sorts of things to misunderstand me and I was very lonely. I just can't stand that loneliness and always being at the point of disappearing. So I'm quite happy screaming and all that, making my presence clear, and it's a healthier thing to do."   (Yoko Ono, 1971)

It's not hard to see that John and Yoko were drawn together through their common bond of loneliness and pain. They also shared an intense creativity and a consuming artist's ego which needs a devoted believer in order to thrive. And despite their inwardness they both had an aptitude for showmanship and public relations which manifested itself in all their activities.

My first impressions of Yoko were that she was a very special person, sometimes forceful and dominating, other times fragile and meek. On the surface she appeared to be a very ambitious woman, a driven, overtly determined artist who was sincerely trying to succeed. One couldn't help but admire her. Her open face would glow, as if revealing some sort of inner knowledge. Her smile could be irresistible, a happy, pleasing smile which made it hard to say no to anything she asked. Yoko could appear so childlike and virginal sitting quietly in a corner somewhere, dressed from head to toe in white, that she might have been mistaken for a teen-age Japanese princess. It was hard to believe she was thirty-four and had a six year old daughter. But occasionally her face would become arrogant when she tilted her head back, letting her long black hair flow behind her, and for all her energy and creativity her life seemed courted by tragedy. I was soon aware that under the facade she was a very unhappy woman.

John Dunbar, the owner of Indica Gallery, who introduced John to Yoko at a preview of her exhibition in November 1966.

Yoko with her "Eternal Time Clock"—a gold clock with no minute hand and no hour hand, just a second hand ticking away counting nothing but the seconds, forever. It was exhibited surrounded by a soundproof perspex box attached to which was a stethoscope, through which you could hear the amplified sounds of the ticking.

Yoko's father had been a successful concert pianist until his father forced him to become a banker and he had to give everything up in the middle of his career. She never saw him until she was three years old and the first thing he did was to examine her hands to see if she would be able to play the piano. Yoko didn't like playing songs on the piano but she loved to compose, which she started to do when she was about five. She would compose songs with little drawings to accompany them and set up children's concerts for her friends.

"It was strange because at the same time they brought me up in such a way to make me feel that I could become somebody important. I think they wanted me to become the first female Prime Minister of Japan, or if not that perhaps a diplomat. What happened was that I began to feel they didn't love me for what I was, so much as they loved me for just being an Ono. They felt I should be proud of it because they were proud of displaying it, and if they could be proud of me, then they wouldn't mind so much having me around."

The war was traumatic for Yoko. She was nine when it began and when the cities were ordered evacuated her parents sent their children and servants out of Tokyo to live in the country. After a while the servants ran away and Yoko found herself having to find food and take care of the younger ones.

"I had to deal with that whole terrible experience *alone.* I'm sure all that made me develop the way I did because I sort of retreated more into myself. I felt the whole thing had been forced on me, and later when I wanted to communicate and express through my art the loneliness and the pain I had felt, nobody understood."

Yoko's family moved to New York in the fifties and she studied composition at Sarah Lawrence College. She was exploring new music and graphic scores but people didn't understand; it was against tradition. Yoko became involved with the avant-garde set, John Cage, the experimental composer, and also Andy Warhol's crowd, but she soon rejected their ideas and went out on her own. She withdrew even more into her closed-up environment and continued the pattern, which would run throughout her life, of living always enclosed with physical limitations.

"I knew then that I was into something special and that was the cause of my loneliness. But the thought of being able to do something, the thought that I may be able to leave a mark on the world excited me tremendously, but can you imagine having all those ideas and nowhere to go with them, nowhere to present them. I knew that I had to communicate my feelings of fear and loneliness that had plagued me all my life, and I felt that the feeling was universal so I had to communicate it."

In the midsixties London had reached its zenith as a vibrant international center of modern art. Its "swinging" image, created by fashion designers, musicians, and youth movements, attracted underground artists from every corner of the world. Art laboratories and underground galleries, which had nothing in common with the established Bond Street "fine art" mausoleums, sprang up overnight to cater to this influx of avant-garders.

By the time Yoko was invited to England in 1966 to attend a symposium on "The Destruction of Art," she had already gained a reputation for herself on the New York art scene for her originality and bizarre events. In London she found the climate receptive to her conceptual style of art, and decided to stay. She soon caught the public eye by calling for volunteers to wrap up one of Landseer's stone lions in Trafalgar Square with a huge white tarpaulin. The sceptical British press was not amused and dismissed the event as a gimmick without even trying to find out her reasons for doing it.

Yoko's "Trafalgar Square Wrapping Event" London, 1966, when she wrapped one of Landseer's stone lions with a white tarpaulin.

Whether Yoko was understood by the press or the general public didn't matter. She was starting to receive favorable reviews in the art magazines before her world collided with John Lennon's. Their first meeting was at the Indica Gallery where Yoko was holding her "Exhibition No. 2." One of the new style galleries, Indica was run by John Dunbar, a Cambridge graduate who was married to the singer Marianne Faithful and friendly with many others in the pop-star elite. The gallery, stuck between a motley assortment of run-down storefronts, was located in Mason's Yard right in the heart of London's West End and reached through a narrow cobblestone alley.

Several versions of their meeting exist. John recalled in *Lennon Remembers:*

"I'd been going around to galleries a bit on my days off in between records. I got the word that this amazing woman was putting on a show next week, and there was going to be something about people in bags, in black bags, and it was going to be a bit of a happening and all that. So I went down to a preview of the show. There was an apple on sale there for two hundred quid. I thought it was fantastic—I got the humour in her work immediately. But there was another piece which really decided me for or against the artist: a ladder which led to a painting which was hung on a ceiling. It looked like a black canvas with a chain and a spy glass hanging on the end of it. I climbed the ladder, looked through the spy

John and Yoko in front of their white Rolls Royce.

glass, and in tiny little letters it said, 'Yes.' So it was positive. I felt relieved. I was very impressed, and John Dunbar sort of introduced us; neither of us knew who the hell we were. And Dunbar had been sort of hustling her, saying 'that's a good patron, you must go and talk to him or do something,' because I was looking for action. John Dunbar insisted she say hello to the millionaire, you know what I mean. And she came up and handed me a card which said, 'Breathe' on it, one of her instructions, so I just went (pant!). This was our meeting!"*

Yoko remembers it slightly differently:

"John asked if he could hammer one of the nails of the 'Hammer-A-Nail-In' piece. It's so symbolic you see; the virginal board, for a man to hammer a nail in. . . . I decided that people should pay five shillings to hammer each nail. But when the gallery owner told John he had to pay, he stopped a moment and asked if he could just hammer an imaginary nail! It was fantastic. It was my game. The two of us were playing the same game. I didn't know who he was. And when I found out I didn't care. I mean, in the art world a Beatle is, well, you know. Also he was in a suit. He looked so ordinary."

In reply to this John added:

"I was in a highly unshaven and tatty state. I was up three nights. I was always up in those days, trippin'. I was stoned. And I wasn't in a suit. That was my psychedelic period!"

Their next meeting was a private showing at another art gallery where Claes Oldenburg's Pop Art drawings were being exhibited. Yoko nodded shyly at John but they hardly spoke. A few weeks later she telephoned him, once for his song scores for a John Cage book, and then again to ask him to back her next exhibition. She sent him a copy of her *Grapefruit* book of instruction poems, from which most of her painting, theater and poetry derives. John kept it by his bed.

"I used to read it sometimes and I'd get very annoyed by it. It would say things like: 'paint until you drop dead,' or 'bleed,' and then sometimes I'd be very enlightened by it, and I went through all the changes that people go through with her work." *

John agreed to finance her "Half-Wind Show" at the underground Lisson Gallery. It was their first public adventure together, and Yoko presented it as: "Yoko Plus Me." John was so uptight about it he didn't even see the show. The exhibition consisted of the most ordinary household furnishings neatly divided in two, painted white, and placed in their traditional settings. There was a bedroom with half a bed on which were half sheets, and half pillows. Half a bedside chair stood beside it and

*Lennon Remembers: The Rolling Stone Interviews, Straight Arrow Books, San Francisco, 1971.

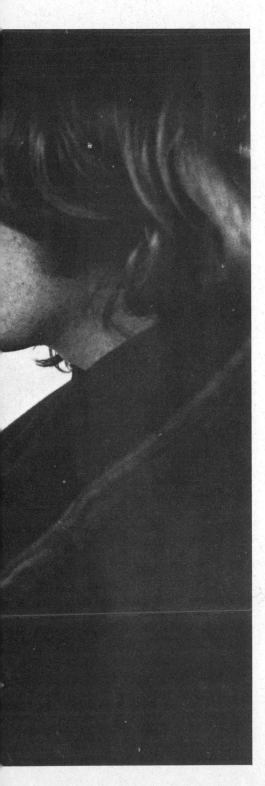

nearby half a washbasin on which lay, of course, half a toothbrush!

Yoko's world fascinated John but the question of whether he really belonged in it worried him: "I'd get very upset about it being intellectual or all fucking avant-garde, then I'd like it, then I wouldn't," he said later.

When Yoko staged her "Dance Event," different cards kept coming through John's door every day, saying: "Breathe," or "Dance," or "Watch all the lights until dawn." They would either depress him or make him ecstatic, depending on his mood.

In February 1968, John left for India with the other Beatles to study transcendental meditation under the Maharishi. Given the time to relax and think about his life he began to realize that he might be in love with Yoko.

"She wrote me all these letters: 'I'm a cloud. Watch for me in the sky.' I'd get so excited about her letters. There was nothin' in them that wives or mothers-in-law could've understood, and from India I started thinkin' of her as a woman, not just an intellectual woman."

Disillusioned with the Maharishi, John felt restless in the mountain retreat. He was also unhappy with his home life. Though he had been aware for some time that his first marriage was just not working he was a coward about it; there was no way he was going to go off and leave Cynthia and his son Julian to be by himself. John explained:

"The way it was with Cyn was she got pregnant, we got married. We never had much to say to each other. But the vibrations didn't upset me because she was quiet, y'know, and I was away all the time. I'd get fed up every now and then, and I'd start this 'where is she?' bit. I'd hope that the 'one' would come. Then I'd get past it. Well, I suppose I was hopin' for a woman who could give me what I got from a man, intellectually. I wanted someone I could be myself with."

John returned from India in April and Yoko began to write him an endless stream of letters, some scribbled on the backs of old envelopes, some many pages long and typed, some exquisitely hand-written on scented notepaper. Bluntly, John was hooked. He finally came to a decision after which there was no looking back. In his own words:

"I called her over. It was the middle of the night, and Cyn was away, and I thought, 'well now's the time if I'm gonna get to know her anymore.' She came to the house and I didn't know what to do, so we went upstairs to my studio and I played her all the tapes that I'd made, some comedy stuff and some electronic music. She was suitably impressed and then she said, 'well let's make one ourselves,' so we made 'Two Virgins.' It was midnight when we started, it was dawn when we finished, and then we made love at dawn. It was very beautiful."*

Yoko describes what happened during their first collaboration:

"This music is a totally new experience for me. John and I did it together. It just happened. It was strict improvisation, no planning. It was a meeting of us, through music, through making music. We were going into an area that none of us really knew. I use voice and John uses everything in the room—old records, piano, percussion. He was operating two tape recorders. He was the busy one. I was just sitting down doing the voice. There's a catch—it's an unfinished music. So if you listen to it maybe you can add to it. Or change it, or edit it—or add something in your mind."

Thus they launched the "Two Virgins" era, an era of fun and moral turpentine, as John once called it. John became the producer of Yoko's art. Yoko became the translator of his fantasies, turning them into "events." And everything they did together was an Event. She taught him abstract art and music. He in turn taught her rock 'n roll. John was possessed; everything he did was dedicated to Yoko. He quickly began to devour all the work she had ever done, an experience which radically affected not only his attitude toward his own work, but more importantly his attitude toward the society in which he lived.

It slowly became apparent, even to the most cynical observers, that John was hopelessly devoted to Yoko, and he didn't care who knew it. It didn't matter how much people abused them, mocked them, laughed at them or wrote them violent letters, because quite simply they were in love.

So lost were they in their love cloud that they were not even aware of the other three Beatles' hostility toward Yoko. Back in the recording studios to work on their next album, Paul and George especially were sceptical about her, and felt she was an intruder. Paul was jealous of Yoko for taking up all of John's time and attention, and he made no bones about the fact that he disliked her. John admitted later in *Lennon Remembers:* "Yoko was naive—she came in and she would expect to perform with them like you would with any group—she was jamming but there was a sort of coldness about it. . . . You see I presumed that I would just be able to carry on and just bring Yoko into our life. But it seemed that I had to either be married to them or Yoko, and I chose Yoko, and I was right."*

John announced his love for Yoko to the public on July 1, 1968, at the opening of his first art exhibition in London's prestigious Robert Frazer Gallery. The show was entitled "You Are Here," and was dedicated "To Yoko from John, With Love." The main exhibit was a large white circular piece of canvas on the center of which was written in John's handwriting:

John and Yoko relax as they photograph themselves with a remote control device for the "Two Virgins" album cover. "For us it was the culmination of our love for one another and of how we thought that love might be useful to others," John said.

*Lennon Remembers: The Rolling Stone Interviews. Straight Arrow Books, San Francisco, 1971.

"You Are Here," John's first art exhibition at the Robert Frazer Gallery, London, which he dedicated "To Yoko from John, with Love." The main exhibit was a white circular canvas in the middle of which was written, in John's handwriting, "You Are Here." To get to the canvas you had to walk through a collection of charity boxes (top right). Outside the gallery John and Yoko released 365 helium-filled white balloons into the sky above Mayfair (above) with a note attached to each balloon saying: "You are here—please write to John Lennon, c/o the Robert Frazer Gallery." John got the idea for the balloons from a childhood memory; he remembered how excited *he* had been when he had found a balloon with a label on it in a field.

Students at the Hornsey College of Art sent John a rusty bike with a tag explaining: "This exhibit was inadvertently left out." John immediately put it in the exhibition (right center). Visitors to the show could leave a contribution, if they so wished, in John's hat (bottom right).

Far right: Frames from a film of the exhibition opening.

"You Are Here." Before a visitor could get near the work, which was downstairs, it was necessary to pass through a huge collection of charity boxes, soliciting funds for a variety of causes ranging from the *National Canine Defense League* to *The Sons of the Divine Providence.*

During the opening the gallery was bursting with press and cameramen, and the colorful array of guests from both the art and pop worlds spilled out onto the pavement. The spectacle took on an even more surreal look when three hundred and sixty-five helium filled white balloons were launched and floated gently up into the sky above Mayfair. Attached to each was a note that read: "You Are Here—please write to John Lennon, c/o The Robert Frazer Gallery, Duke Street, London, W.1." Replies to the invitation came in by the hundreds, objecting to John's upcoming divorce from Cynthia, his association with Yoko, his wealth, his long hair, and his presumption at stepping into the preserve of art. John was genuinely surprised by the attack. "The trouble, I suppose," he said, "is that I've spoiled my image. People want me to stay in their own bag. They want me to be lovable. But I was never that. Even at school I was just 'Lennon.' Nobody ever thought of me as cuddly!"

Critical reaction to the show was unexpectedly cold. Discussing this John said: "Putting it on was taking a swipe at them in a way. I mean that's what it was about. A lot of them were saying, 'well, if that hadn't been by John Lennon nobody would have gone to it,' but it was *me* doing it. And they're using that to say it didn't work. Work as what?"

Yoko said: "People thought there should be something more to the show. Someone wrote saying: 'that's not even Pop Art, it's Lollypop Art.' Well that's beautiful. I thought that was a compliment. The show was John's idea. Many people think that any crazy idea John gets is connected with me. Actually John has all these crazy ideas all the time. He just didn't use them. It was just a personal joke for himself. He has about twenty ideas in twenty minutes. He just goes on talking about an idea. So I say: 'well, that idea is good, why don't you just do it?,' and he had never thought of actually doing it, physically. The point is, when you do something, something happens, the concept is simple, but then you get all sorts of reactions and you've started something."

The events of the next few months were tragic and did much harm to the already vulnerable couple. Their love cloud slowly disintegrated and harsh reality intervened.

Just before midday on October 18, 1968, John and Yoko were awakened by loud shouting and the noise of someone battering the front

John and Yoko surrounded by police and jostled by a crowd of 300 outside Marylebone Magistrate's Court after the drug arrest hearing.

door of Ringo's basement apartment, where they were staying, in London's Montague Square. It took John five minutes to get out of bed and get to the door to see what all the banging was about. He opened it to confront Detective-Sergeant Norman Pilcher of the Scotland Yard Drugs Squad.

An hour later John, dressed in a black hip-length Salvation Army coat and black bell bottom trousers, and Yoko, dressed in a shorty fur coat and trousers, were marched off by a policewoman in plain clothes and six other policemen to a row of waiting police cars. At Paddington Green police station they were charged with unlawful possession of cannabis resin and also with willfully obstructing the police in the execution of their search warrant.

"It was the most terrifying experience I have ever had," said John afterwards. He and Yoko appeared in court the following day at Marylebone Magistrate's Court and were let out on bail. A crowd of three hundred jostled the police who stood shoulder to shoulder to protect them as they entered and left the courthouse.

John pleaded guilty so that the police would not press charges against Yoko and she would get off. Little did he realize the repercussions this decision would have years later, when he wanted desperately to live in New York. John swore later that the lump of hash had been planted in their apartment because neither he nor Yoko were taking any drugs at the time and they had only been living there a few months. It was a well-known fact that Pilcher was out for promotion and he was later arrested and subsequently suspended from his job.

In the House of Commons, Mr. Arthur Lewis, a Labour Member of Parliament, asked the Home Secretary why it had been necessary to employ such a large task force to carry out a comparatively simple duty. And why all the police dogs and their helpers? The Home Secretary, Mr. Callaghan, replied that the police considered the twelve persons involved an adequate force and deemed the dogs necessary since they had been specially trained to detect cannabis. The total cost of the police operation had been one hundred and seventy-eight pounds, one shilling and seven pence.

Several months earlier John's wife Cynthia had announced that she was suing for divorce, the grounds being his adultery with Yoko, which at the time John denied. When the divorce was heard in court on November 8, he decided not to defend the case, which was probably wise because the previous week Yoko had been admitted to the hospital for various blood transfusions. It was revealed that she was pregnant and expecting John's child a few days after Christmas. While the divorce hearing

John stayed with Yoko in Queen Charlotte's Maternity Hospital where she suffered a miscarriage. When the spare bed was needed he slept on the floor in a sleeping bag.

was going on John was camped in a sleeping bag at the side of Yoko's bed in Queen Charlotte's Maternity Hospital.

Captain Henry Kirby, a Conservative Member of Parliament, complained about John's invasion of the hospital's privacy. John had to be defended by the Minister of Health himself, who replied that it was quite commonplace for Queen Charlotte's Hospital to "'allow a prospective father to attend confinement and to be present at delivery, unless asked to leave by a doctor."

John's solicitor, David Jacobs, negotiated a very advantageous financial settlement for Cynthia with her lawyers. Tony Cox, Yoko's husband, said that John was "a great guy—they have my best wishes," and John recorded the baby's heartbeat for posterity. But tragedy struck when Yoko suffered a miscarriage the day after the divorce. John, who was still awaiting a hearing on the drug charge, was totally devastated by the disaster and for days shut himself off from everybody and everything. "Babies make the world happier and that's our scene," he had said when he first found out that Yoko was pregnant.

Three weeks later, in Criminal Court, John was fined one hundred and fifty pounds plus twenty guineas costs, after he had pleaded guilty to being in unauthorized possession of two hundred and nineteen grains of cannabis resin (enough for about forty joints). He took full responsibility as had been arranged, and Yoko was discharged.

Ironically, in the face of mounting public criticism and continuous abuse from British newspapers, John and Yoko, in a determined mood, chose this very moment to release "Two Virgins," the record they made their first night together, with an explicitly nude album cover. As if they didn't have enough problems the album was released on November 29, the same day as John's drug conviction. It seemed to many that John was trying very hard to lose whatever following he still had left and that he would be the first rock 'n' roll superstar to be destroyed by public ridicule.

The "Two Virgins" album was an abstract collage of electronics and cinema verité noises. It was used for the soundtrack of John and Yoko's film of the same name. Originally John had planned it as Yoko's record alone, and he intended to have her nude on the cover "because her work is naked, basically simple and childlike and truthful." The English music papers described it as "the most talked about non-musical event of the year."

The pictures were taken with a remote control device by John himself, in Ringo's basement apartment. "I was a little startled," he said, describing his first reaction to the photographs. "I mean, there I was, all of me, in a photo, and I thought, 'Ah ha! there might just be trouble with this one!' "

There was trouble. The first few printers approached to do the jacket refused. Once it was printed E.M.I., the conglomerate that held exclusive rights to Beatles records, refused to handle it, and advertisements for the record were refused by all the leading pop music papers. They even refused to use a special cartoon that John had drawn as an alternative to the nude photos. A small British firm called Track Records took on the project and distributed the record in a plain brown wrapper. Similarly in the United States Capitol Records refused to touch it, and it was handled by a company called Tetragammation. Thirty thousand copies of the record were impounded at Newark, New Jersey, because the police claimed the covers were pornographic.

"The picture was to prove that we are not a couple of demented freaks and that we are not deformed in any way and that our minds are healthy. If you think that it was obscene, it can only have been so in your own mind. For us it was the culmination of our love for one another and of how we thought that love might be useful to others," John said in answer to the critics, adding: "If we can make society accept that we are in love and therefore they should stop sniggering at us, we shall be achieving our purpose." A week after the release of the record, *Smile* and *Two Virgins*, the first two films that John and Yoko had made together, were given their world premiere at the Chicago Film Festival. Shot in super-eight, they were made in the spirit of home movies, and both were filmed in the garden at Kenwood. *Smile* consists of a soft focused single shot of John's face, smiling. It took only three minutes to shoot but was slowed down to last fifty-two minutes by using a high-speed camera which could take twenty thousand frames per minute. *Two Virgins* was shot at a much slower speed although it still retains a form of slow motion. It also uses John's face, this time superimposed on Yoko's, to give the impression of seeing Yoko through John's eyes, or John smiling with Yoko's mouth. The film runs for nineteen minutes; toward the end the two images slowly separate and John and Yoko embrace.

"In both films we were mainly concerned about the vibrations the films send out, and the kind that was between us," explained Yoko.

John said: "The film works with somebody else smiling—Yoko went into all that. It originally started out that she wanted a million people all over the world to send in a snapshot of themselves smiling, and then it got down to lots of people smiling, and then maybe one or two, and then me smiling as a symbol of today smiling—and that's what I am, whatever that means. And so it's me smiling and that's the hangup of course because it's me again. But I mean they've got to see it someday—it's only

Yoko in front of a frame from *Smile*, one of the first films she made with John. The film consists of a soft focused single shot of John's face, smiling. It only took three minutes to shoot but was slowed down to last fifty-two minutes by using a high-speed camera.

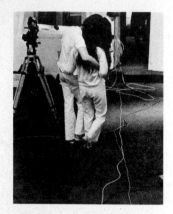

Constantly together, John and
Yoko leave Twickenham Studios after
a day's filming of "Let It Be."

me. I don't mind if people go to the film to see me smiling because you
see it's not that harmful. The idea of the film won't really be dug for
another fifty or a hundred years probably. That's what it's all about. I just
happen to be that face."

Nineteen sixty-nine started out badly for John. After the unhappiness
and crises of the preceding months he had given little if any thought to
the Beatles or to Beatle music. He was totally involved with Yoko, their
projects and their problems. When Paul decided that it was time for
another Beatle movie or perhaps for the group to go on the road, John
just didn't want to know. But under constant pressure from Paul,
John finally wasn't strong enough to say no as he later admitted in
Lennon Remembers:

"He [Paul] sort of set it up, and there were discussions about where to
go and all of that, and I would just tag along . . . I had Yoko and I didn't
even give a shit about nothin'. I was stoned all the time and I just didn't
give a shit, you know."*

Both John and George were fed up with being side men for Paul, who
had arranged "Let It Be" to suit himself. To complicate matters Yoko
was treated in a very insulting way by everybody involved in the production, including the other Beatles and their wives. She was at John's side
for the whole of the filming and at one point joined in a group jam, but
later Paul deliberately had the footage cut out of the film.

The whole episode was a bad experience for John. He remembered
sadly: "Paul had this idea that he was going to rehearse us. He's looking
for perfection all the time, and so he has these ideas that we should rehearse and then make the album . . . We put down a few tracks and
nobody was into it at all. I don't know, it was just a dreadful, dreadful feeling in Twickenham Studios, and being filmed all the time, you know. I
just wanted them to go away. And we'd be there at eight in the morning,
and you couldn't make music at eight in the morning or ten, or whatever it was, in a strange place with people filming you and colored lights."*

When it was finished there were twenty-nine hours of tape that nobody
wanted to touch. They sat on a shelf collecting dust and John felt so ve-
hemently about them that he described them as "the shittiest load of
badly recorded shit with a lousy feeling to it ever."*

By comparison, John's first excursion into avant-garde music with Yoko
at a concert of experimental jazz in Cambridge was an exhilarating experience. The event happened at a March Sunday afternoon concert at
the Lady Mitchell Hall. A dozen international jazzmen had made a three

*Lennon Remembers: The Rolling Stone Interviews. Straight Arrow Books, San Francisco, 1971.

hour assault on the audience, in a gigantic improvisational session. Then John and Yoko, who had been waiting in the wings, strolled out to meet the audience. The local Cambridge newspaper described the scene: "Miss Ono began with a fearsome siren note, as Japanese as a Noh Play Chant, and sustained it to the point of self-torture. Lennon was squatting at her feet, back to the audience, holding, shaking, swinging electric guitars right up against a large speaker, or hitting the instrument against the speaker, to create ear-splitting feedbacks. . . . The concert was strange and chilling, not in a bad sense, but because so much unusual sound texture and harsh melody were disturbing. At no time did the music become comforting. It was an extraordinary experience."

John said: "What she'd done for the guitar playing was to free it the way she'd freed her voice from all the restrictions. I was always thinking, 'well I can't quite play like Eric or George, or B. B. King,' but then I gave up trying to play like that and just played whatever I could, whatever way I could, to match it to her voice."

Although John was no longer getting anything out of the Beatles artistically, Yoko was turning him on to a million things. During their first year together they experienced an incredible series of highs and lows, sharing a spiritual and artistic awareness despite repeated exposure to other people's scepticism and ridicule. Before he met Yoko, John had been a walking cocoon, alienated and withdrawn, dropping acid almost constantly. Even the fragmentary lyrics of his songs reflected this confusion. He had become the Nin character who flung himself from heights, intent on catching the swing midway but fearful of the fatal slip into abysms. Yoko showed John a language, a way of life built on instinct, emotion and intuition—the most inarticulate parts of himself. She showed John that art is the most effective way of overcoming human resistance to truth. She revealed to him a new dimension, setting in motion an inner transformation which eventually reversed his role of the *nowhere man* wanting to be completely left alone, to that of the *communicator* always ready to project outward.

Yoko's most important influence on John was in showing him that he was an artist, in the all-encompassing sense of the word, and that as such he could broaden his creative horizons in unlimited directions. And he affected her too. Their elemental chemistry combined to make each a stronger, more aware person, and it was this chemistry which fostered the conditions for *growth*. With the coming-together of yin and yang— the complementary spirits of John and Yoko—a pattern of energy was invoked, irreversible and indestructible.

WAR IS OVER!

IF YOU WANT IT

Happy Christmas from John & Yoko

THE PEACE POLITICIAN

THE BED-INS—AMSTERDAM AND MONTREAL

"The actual peace event we staged came directly from Yoko. She had decided that whatever action she took, she took for a specific reason. Her reason was peace. I'd been singing about love, which I guess was another word for peace. Our actual peace demonstrations were Yoko-style events. They were also pure theatre. The Bed sit-in in Canada was one of the nicest ones, and I participated almost like a spectator because it was Yoko's way of demonstrating."   (John Lennon, 1975)

Once Yoko had shown John a way in which they could demonstrate, he was able to use all his influence as a Beatle and as a public figure, enhanced, of course, by his beguiling rhetoric, his tremendous reserve of energy and capacity for endurance. John's motive was primarily to do something constructive with the constant publicity given to anything and everything he did. Their objective was to turn the Bed-In into an event that would have maximum effect through the widest coverage.

"We worked for three months thinking out the most functional approach to boosting peace before we got married, and spent our honeymoon talking to the press in bed in Amsterdam," Yoko explained. "For us, it was the only way. We can't go out in Trafalgar Square because it would create a riot. We can't lead a parade or a march because of all the autograph hunters. We had to find our own way of doing it, and for now Bed-Ins seem to be the most logical way. We think the Bed-In can be effective."

The first Bed-In took place after John and Yoko's secret marriage in Gibraltar on March 20, 1969. They picked Gibraltar after having tried to get married everywhere else first, and also, John said, because it was quiet, friendly, and British. Two days later they were ensconced in Suite 902 of the Amsterdam Hilton and word quickly got out that the Lennons were spending seven days of their honeymoon in bed for peace and as a protest against all forms of violence. The world's press were formally invited to interview them to discuss their campaign.

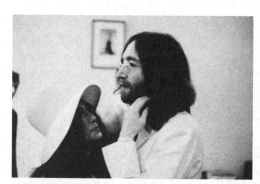 

John and Yoko's wedding day on the Rock of
Gibraltar, March 20, 1969. Above top: In the back of
the limousine on the way to the ceremony, after
flying for three hours from Paris. Above center: In
the Registrar's office signing the official book.
Bottom left: John, ecstatic, on the plane
back to Paris.

The wedding ceremony: John puts the ring on
Yoko's finger. Standing next to them is the Registrar,
Cecil Wheeler.

Now married, John and Yoko stand outside the
British Consulate building.

Identically dressed in white robes, John and Yoko sat in an enormous king size bed in the Grand Bedroom of the Presidential Suite, surrounded by flowers, posters, and drawings. The walls were covered with hand-painted signs reading "Bed Peace," "Hair Peace," "I love John" and "I love Yoko." On the first day alone there were over fifty journalists, photographers, disc jockeys, and camera crews, all anxious to find out what was happening. John was confident but emotional; conjuring, compelling, words flowed ceaselessly from the magic Lennon tongue. His outward appearance was commanding. From John's ever changing gallery of faces an image had evolved that perfectly suited this new role: long flowing hair framing the intense bearded face, accentuating his glazed eyes behind the National Health round wire glasses, the tautness and seriousness of his features alternating with the familiar leery smile. When he spoke he manipulated his hands in sharp gestures typical of his vibrant body language:

"We are both artists! Peace is our art. We believe that because of everything I was as a Beatle and everything that we are now, we stand a chance of influencing other young people. And it is they who will rule the world tomorrow."

For seven days, from ten in the morning until ten in the evening, John and Yoko talked nonstop about peace. Planeloads of journalists flew in to cover the event and were for the most part sceptical. Half of them had expected to see the couple making love in front of the cameras; when they were confronted with a barrage of serious peace slogans they were disappointed. The attitude of the British press in particular was harsh and critical, and the way in which they hurled abuse, mercilessly lampooning John and Yoko, was unnecessary and deliberately hurtful. Nevertheless, John's message did get printed, most often with a large amount of space given to photographs accompanied by the gist of his conversation.

"We're very shy and straight and ordinary," John said in an effort to explain his feelings. "We're just trying to do the best we can. But we're in an abnormal situation. The Blue meanies, or whoever they are, are promoting violence all the time in every newspaper, every TV show and every magazine. The least Yoko and I can do is hog the headlines and make people laugh. I'd sooner see our faces in a bed in the paper than yet another politician smiling at the people and shaking hands."

Apart from becoming physically exhausted John enjoyed the Bed-In, and the energy and attention that surrounded it. "It's the best idea we've had yet," he said. "Better than wriggling about in a black bag or stripping naked for people who don't appreciate what we're trying to do or why. Just suppose we had wanted to go to Capri for a secret honeymoon like

John and Yoko at the foot of the stairs after the wedding ceremony, surrounded by the staff of the British Consulate.

Jackie Kennedy had, the press would have been bound to find out. So we thought we might as well do something constructive about the publicity.''

Although the main impetus for and visualization of the Bed-Ins came from Yoko, and related more to the personalities of John and Yoko than to the peace movement in general, John had been gradually influenced by the political consciousness of the sixties, particularly the London Underground.

Frame from a video film of John and Yoko in a bag, onstage at the Royal Albert Hall during the Alchemical Wedding.

The Underground was a diverse group embracing all manner of artists, beats, mystics and freaks, and John went out of his way to contribute to their media—especially the newspaper *International Times* (later *IT*). He had been confronted at various times by several prominent members of this community, who had asked him pointedly what *he* was doing about peace, and he had especially taken to heart a letter from Peter Watkins, the controversial filmmaker, repeating this question. Many smaller incidents had also registered with John. At the Alchemical Wedding, for instance, which was the Underground's Christmas party in 1968, a gray-suited politico, waving a banner about Biafra, had screamed: ''Do you care John Lennon, do you care?'' while John and Yoko were on-stage in a bag.

Whether he liked it or not, John played a leading role in the youth movement. Being a Beatle had originally placed him in the part but his own actions had validated his position. Certainly in the eyes of the public John represented the left-wing, political aspect of the group. His widely publicized comments on Christianity and the Beatles, though completely misunderstood, were basic statements of fact reflecting the sentiments of most youth on the current state of religion. In turn, youth had followed John and the other Beatles in their experimentation with drugs, and their quest for cosmic consciousness with the Maharishi. What developed was a kind of mutual interaction between John and his audience, which he tried to influence through the Bed-Ins and later through his music.

John always had political opinions and had been satirizing the system ever since he wrote for and distributed outspoken magazines in school. He had grown up very aware of his working-class origins: ''It's pretty basic when you're brought up like I was, to hate and fear the police as a natural enemy and to despise the army as something that takes everybody away and leaves them dead somewhere. It's just a basic working class thing, though it begins to wear off as you get older and get a family and get swallowed up by the system.''

John's class consciousness never did really wear off, but of course it did

get overshadowed at the height of Beatlemania. Working at a phe-
nomenal pace, constantly touring, he had little chance to express his true
feelings, and felt constantly pressured by his Beatle "image." When after
a couple of American tours Epstein tried to persuade the group to say
nothing about Vietnam, John finally countered: "Listen, when they ask
next time, we're gonna say we don't like that war and we think they
should get right out!" As he explained it: "The continual awareness of
what was going on made me feel ashamed I wasn't saying anything. I
burst out because I could no longer play that game any more—it was just
too much for me."

The Bed-Ins were immensely important to John, since they provided the
release he needed for accumulated passions and emotionally charged
political feelings that had been building up inside him for so long. It was a
lonely and brave stand to take and he was prepared to put his credibility
on the line. Besides Yoko, there was literally nobody else who supported
his actions or stood by him. To do what John did, and to pull through all
the humiliation involved, it was necessary that he have complete faith in
himself. "Yoko and I are quite willing to be the world's clowns," he said,
"if by so doing it will do some good. I know I'm one of these 'famous
personalities.' For reasons only known to themselves, people do print
what I say. And I'm saying peace. We're not pointing a finger at anybody. There are no good guys and bad guys. The struggle is in the mind.
We must bury our own monsters and stop condemning people. We are
all Christ and we are all Hitler. We want Christ to win. We're trying to
make Christ's message contemporary. What would he have done if he
had advertisements, records, films, TV and newspapers? Christ made
miracles to tell his message. Well, the miracle today is communications,
so let's use it."

Protests were raised about the cost of the Bed-In, the extravagance of the
Hilton Hotel luxury suite, the money for which could perhaps have been
used in a more practical way. John was adamant, however, on that point:
"People criticized us for spending all that money protesting about Biafra
and suchlike, when the money would have been more useful had I sent it
directly there. But I'd already done that. And I have always respected the
sentiments behind that kind of charity and I always will do. But it doesn't
solve the problem. . . . In a capitalist society like ours, people are much
more effective if they have money. And we have. Our name is known
and so we're using our fame and our money to advertise for peace.
Some people say that that is a pretentious ambition but we feel that the
big problems are where you've got to start. . . ."

The Amsterdam Bed-In was a beginning, a sort of trial run for John and

The Montreal Bed-In: John and Yoko gave over sixty interviews to the media, talked to hundreds of radio stations all over America and recorded "Give Peace A Chance"—all from their bed in the Queen Elizabeth Hotel.

Yoko to feel their way around and see how much they could accomplish with this type of hard-sell campaign. They felt the event was successful mainly because it did get their message plastered all over the front pages of the world's newspapers. For John it was the start of a spiraling manic devotion to the peace cause, which led him into frenzied attempts at all-out media saturation.

By the time of the Montreal Bed-In two months after Amsterdam, John and Yoko were more self-assured and glowing with supercharged energy. They were ready to take on North America. As veterans of the "sell peace" campaign, with the echo of a thousand interviews behind them, they now faced the biggest challenge of their chosen career. They had desperately tried to gain entry into the United States, but each time John's visa had been denied. Rather than wait any longer, they decided on the practical strategy of staging a second Bed-In close enough to talk to the U.S. media, and generate a flood of publicity. They arrived in Canada after finding the Bahamas totally unsuitable. It was midnight on Monday, May 26, 1969, when John and Yoko and their entourage checked into the Queen Elizabeth Hotel in Montreal. After much aggravation with immigration authorities they were granted a ten-day stay, during which time they were to give over sixty interviews to the press.

Inside their crowded suite John and Yoko sat peacefully holding hands, surrounded by pink and white carnations, record players, film equipment, and busy phones. They were both relaxed and at ease with reporters. "The whole effect of our Bed-In has made people talk about peace," John said. "We're trying to interest young people into doing something for peace. But it must be done by nonviolent means—otherwise there can only be chaos. We're saying to the young people—and they have always been the hippest ones—we're telling them to get the message across to the squares. A lot of young people have been ignoring the squares when they should be helping them. The whole scene has become too serious and too intellectual."

"What about talking to the people who make the decisions, the power brokers?" suggested a cynical reporter. John laughed, "Shit, talk? Talk about what? It doesn't happen like that. In the U.S., the Government is too busy talking about how to keep me out. If I'm a joke, as they say, and not important, why don't they just let me in?"

From their bed John spent a lot of time on the phone talking with AM and FM radio stations all around the United States and Canada. His energy seemed to be unlimited, and he kept up a more or less constant conversation, one call after another, all the time promoting peace. The immediacy of his rhetoric was put to the test when he was connected to students who were in the midst of a Peoples' Park demonstration in Berkeley. They were emotionally worked up and scared about a show-down with the police. "Help us, what are we going to do? It's going to go wrong!" they shouted. With understanding and persuasiveness in his voice, John replied: "There's no cause worth losing your life for, there isn't any path worth getting shot for and you can do better by moving on to another city. . . . Don't move about if it aggravates the pigs, and don't get hassled by the cops, and don't play their games. I know it's hard—Christ you know it ain't easy, you know how hard it can be man, so what? Everything's hard—it's better to have it hard than to not have it at all!" John worked himself up into a fury: "Entice them, entice them! Con them—you've got the brains, you can do it. You can make it, man! We can make it—together. We can get it—together!"

At times like this, I felt his peace campaign was working. The personal contacts and exchanges were worth so much more than any photo in a newspaper. More important, he was getting his message over to the kids who needed his advice, and who really believed in him.

For a long time, John had been thinking about using his music to pro-mote peace. On the final weekend of the Bed-In, between eight in the evening Saturday, and three the next morning, John led everyone in the Montreal hotel room in singing his newly written "Give Peace A Chance." It was a rousing song with a simple, catchy message, a perfect expression of John's feelings. An eight-track portable recording machine was hauled to the hotel to record it. The chorus included comedian Tommy Smothers, Timothy Leary and his wife Rosemary, Rabbi Abraham L. Feinberg and the Canadian chapter of the Radha Krishna Temple.

"Give Peace A Chance" was spontaneous and improvised. It was perhaps the most important contribution John could give to the peace movement, and the phrase "we don't have a leader but now we have a song" was soon echoed all over America.

THE MEDIA SATURATION CAMPAIGN

"Henry Ford knew how to sell cars by advertising. I'm selling peace, and Yoko and I are just one big advertising campaign. It may make people laugh but it may make them think, too. Really, we're Mr. and Mrs. Peace."   (John Lennon, 1969)

After the success of the Montreal Bed-In, John began his media satura-tion campaign, giving daily interviews to as many people as possible in his promotion of peace. This dialogue with the press became a way of life. Whenever he felt they were losing interest or that the cam-

John and Yoko, Ralph Ginsburg, editor of *Avant Garde*, and his wife, and Anthony Fawcett hold up "War Is Over" posters during the visit to Toronto.

paign in general was losing its impetus, he would think up an event to stimulate renewed attention. The campaign stretched over a torturous nine months from April to December 1969, with a short break during the summer when John and Yoko had a car accident in Scotland, and the Beatles recorded "Abbey Road."

The center of activity was John and Yoko's office at Apple, where interviews were scheduled at half-hour intervals, often as many as fifteen in a single day. John and Yoko's determination amazed me—they seemed always happy to repeat the same messages and answer the same questions. Everyone went into high gear to keep up this pace; excitement and energy seemed to bounce all over the place. The reception area and Derek Taylor's press office were always spilling over with media people waiting for their turn to be escorted to John and Yoko's office.

"All I'm trying to do is make people aware that it is they themselves who have the power," John told the journalists. "It is the people themselves who must take the initiative, and especially so if the Government does not. And the way to mobilize this power is not through the use of violence. . . . I'm often asked what I would replace all the mess that we have now with. My answer to that is people. Just the idea that the individual is capable of looking after himself, that we don't need centralized government, that we don't need father-figures and leaders, that every child is an artist until he's told he's not an artist, that every person is great until some demagogue makes him less great. Government was an invention that I think didn't work."

One effect of all the exposure was that the United States press began to report more favorably about John; there was some concern as to why he was not being allowed into the country to demonstrate for peace. "I'm sure we'll get there," John said. "It's just a matter of under what conditions. We won't play games with the gov'ments."

Having decided that John was serious about his peace crusade, the U.S. press was particularly interested in reporting his distress about student violence: "The students are being conned!" John said. "It's like the school bully—he aggravates you and aggravates you until you hit him, and then they kill you like in Berkeley. Establishment—it's just a name for evil. The monster doesn't care. . . . The Blue Meanies are insane. We really care about life. Destruction is good enough for the Establishment. The only thing they can't control is the mind, and we have to fight for sanity and peace on that level. But the students have gotten conned into thinking you can change it with violence, and you can't, you know—that can only make it uglier and worse."

In his Apple office John holds up his letters to the Prime Minister, Harold Wilson, and the Queen, informing them that he is returning his M.B.E. medal ''in protest against Britain's involvement in the Nigeria-Biafra thing, against our support of America in Vietnam, and against 'Cold Turkey' slipping down the charts.'' John signed his letters, ''With love, John Lennon of Bag.''

After a while the constant demands of the media campaign began to affect both John and Yoko. Their relationship became increasingly emotionally strained; out of the office tempers flared. I felt that the pace might have eased off had it not been for the growing responsibility John assumed to "produce peace." This was a distinct reversal; in the past he had always been quick to avoid any responsibility at all. John wrote to Bertrand Russell, pleading with him to help their campaign. He told Russell that he didn't think peace was fashionable anymore and that youth was shouting, "Kill the pigs." He felt that he and Yoko could change this, and all the quicker if Russell helped.

John had been waiting for the right moment to send his M.B.E. (the Member of the British Empire medal which had been awarded each of the Beatles in 1965) back to the Queen. In November 1969, aggravated by escalation of the war in Vietnam and the war in Biafra, he decided to stage the event to bring attention to the wars as well as to infuse new energy into the peace campaign.

After breakfast November 26 was to be the day. John rushed downstairs and told Les, the chauffeur, to leave right away for his Aunt Mimi's house in Bournemouth to bring the medal back off the top of her TV set. Meanwhile, John, Yoko and I left to drive to the Apple office. John curled up in the back seat, pondering how to phrase his letter to the Queen, laughing as we all contributed ideas. He asked me to buzz Derek Taylor as soon as we reached the office and tell him to be prepared for an important press release within the hour. Once in our office, John immediately sat down to write out a rough draft of the letter. When it was finished he handed it to me to get it typed up on "Bag Productions" stationery. It read: "Your Majesty, I am returning this M.B.E. in protest against Britain's involvement in the Nigeria-Biafra thing, against our support of America in Vietnam, and against ' Cold Turkey ' slipping down the charts. With Love, John Lennon of Bag."

The letter, together with the medal in a plain white envelope, was delivered in John's new six-door white Mercedes limousine to the tradesmen's entrance of Buckingham Palace. A copy was also sent to the Prime Minister at Number Ten Downing Street. An hour later the official Apple press release was sent out and Derek Taylor was contacting every media person imaginable.

John decided to have an immediate press conference and within minutes our office was crowded with television news cameramen, radio interviewers, photographers, and all the Fleet Street newspaper heavies. John and Yoko, both dressed in black, sat behind their desk, and John read his statement as the cameras whirred. "I'd been planning it for over a year," he told everybody. "I was waiting for a time to do it."

Later that evening after the pressure had died down and the phones had stopped ringing, we relaxed in the office. Yoko lay down on the couch and went to sleep and John turned on the television just in time to catch his interview on the six o'clock news. He was happy. The next day, however, the newspapers took the opportunity to hammer at John again for his gimmickry, and were especially critical of his reference to "Cold Turkey." He had put this in the letter mainly to take the pompousness out of an otherwise formal event, but that simple explanation was ignored. A spokesman from Buckingham Palace said it was ironic "that *he* should return the medal, as the first M.B.E.s that were returned were from people protesting that Mr. Lennon and the other Beatles were given the award in the first place."

John explained further: "Of course my action was a publicity gimmick for peace. I always squirmed when I saw M.B.E. on my letters. I didn't really belong to that sort of world. I think the Establishment bought the Beatles with it. Now I am giving it back, thank you very much. Investitures are a waste of time. It's mostly hypocritical snobbery and part of the class system. I only took it to help the Beatles make the big time. I know I sold my soul when I received it, but now I have helped to redeem it in the cause of peace." With regard to his reference to "Cold Turkey," he said: "When we thought of that we were screaming with laughter, and so a few snobs and hypocrites got very upset about mentioning 'Cold Turkey' with the problem of Biafra and Vietnam, but that saved it from being too serious and being another Colonel protesting! You have to try and do everything with humour, and keep smiling."

The Palace put the medal in a drawer for safekeeping.

"I don't think the Queen will be embarrassed," John said.

"The Queen is above embarrassment," replied a Palace spokesman.

A letter arrived from Bertrand Russell, saying that he was very pleased to see in the press John's strong condemnation of the British Government's role in the wars of Vietnam and Biafra. "Whatever abuse you have suffered in the press as a result of this," he wrote, "I am confident that your remarks will have caused a very large number of people to think again about these wars."

After the M.B.E. event, John and Yoko put all their energy into organizing the "War Is Over" campaign. They had decided on a special

Christmas message: "War Is Over—If you want it—Happy Christmas, John and Yoko," that was to appear on huge billboards erected in twelve cities around the world, and on thousands of posters distributed in the suburbs. Yanou Collart, a top Parisian public relations person, arranged to have the French billboards placed in prominent positions on the Champs Elysées and in several other Paris locations. Similar arrangements were made for Rome, Berlin, Athens, Tokyo, New York, Los Angeles, Toronto, Montreal, and Port-of-Spain in Trinidad.

To launch the campaign, on December 15, 1969 John played at a "Peace For Christmas" charity concert, held at the Lyceum Theatre on behalf of the United Nations Children's Fund. Behind the stage a huge "War Is Over" billboard was erected. John had got together the nucleus of the Plastic Ono Band—Alan White on drums and Klaus Voormann, bass, and he had asked George Harrison, who had been performing with Delaney and Bonnie, to come join them. Right up to the last minute we didn't know if he would come. From the miniscule upstairs dressing room at the Lyceum, I called to find out what was happening, and was informed that everybody was on the way. Ten minutes later George appeared along with Eric Clapton, the complete Delaney and Bonnie Band, Billy Preston, and Keith Moon.

It was the first time in four years that two Beatles had played together in public, and the expanded group immediately became known as the Plastic Ono Supergroup. Crowding the stage they launched into an all-out version of "Cold Turkey," and followed with a climactic seventeen-minute rendering of Yoko's "Don't Worry Kyoko." Yoko had been sitting at John's feet on the stage, covered by a white bag, but when they began this song she got up and started her piercing, shrill screams, interjecting shouts of "You killed Hanratty!" It was an incredible performance, and when it was over everybody stumbled back to the dressing room exhausted.

"War Is Over" was an effective campaign and the culmination of John and Yoko's attempt at media saturation. Its very internationalism was impressive and the billboards drew positive response from the public in every city.

CANADA: THE PEACE FESTIVAL AND PRIME MINISTER TRUDEAU

Snow was falling when John, Yoko, and I arrived at Ronnie Hawkins' farmhouse in the countryside outside Toronto. The day before our arrival, December 15, the city had been plastered with thousands of "War Is Over" posters, and thirty roadside billboards.

John and Yoko's international "War Is Over" billboard campaign was launched on December 15, 1969, in twelve cities around the world carrying the message: "War Is Over—If You Want It—Happy Christmas from John and Yoko." Top left: The billboard high above Hollywood's Sunset Strip; center left: Above the freeway in Toronto; bottom left: Sticking up posters all over the suburbs; top right and opposite page: The posters all over Toronto; center right: Ritchie Yorke and Ronnie Hawkins take the message all the way to the Chinese border in Hong Kong.

During John and Yoko's stay at the Hawkins' farmhouse outside Toronto. Standing left to right: Yoko, Ronnie Hawkins, John, Dick Gregory and Wanda Hawkins (top).

John and Yoko skidooing (bottom).

The visit to Canada had been arranged by John Brower, who had previously organized John's successful appearance at the Toronto Rock 'n' Roll Festival, and Ritchie Yorke, an industrious rock writer whom John trusted. They had visited us at Apple twelve days earlier to discuss their idea for a "bigger than Woodstock" Peace Festival, which included establishing a Peace Foundation. Also, meeting with Pierre Trudeau seemed a serious possibility.

The first press conference was held at the Ontario Science Centre with more than fifty reporters in attendance. John spoke slowly and confidently: "We've come back to Canada to announce plans for a big peace and musical festival to be held at Mosport Park near Toronto on July 3rd, 4th, and 5th next year. We aim to make it the biggest music festival in history, and we're going to be asking everybody who's anybody to play. . . . Along with the festival, we are going to have an International Peace Vote. We're asking everyone to vote for either peace or war and to send in a coupon with their name and address. This is going to be done worldwide through music papers initially, and when we've got about 20 million votes, we're going to give them to the United States. It's just another positive step."

Back at the Hawkins' French provincial hideaway John and Yoko began four days of intense peace campaigning; three extra phones were installed and the house became a temporary relay station. Calls were placed to radio networks all over America; these were interspersed with many personal interviews. The household grew: two macrobiotic cooks were hired, Dick Gregory came to stay and entertained everybody with his biting commentaries. Ray Connolly, the English journalist, arrived from London, and Ralph Ginsberg, Editor of *Avant-Garde* magazine, turned up with Publisher Bob LeShuffy to discuss erotic lithograph spin-offs.

Amidst all this craziness John somehow managed to relax (and even get some kicks), cruising up and down the snow-covered hills on Ronnie's Ski-Doos and Amphicats. Each afternoon he bundled up in an army sergeant's shirt, thick black pants, long rubber boots, and a balaclava, then rushed outside to race across the open fields at seventy miles an hour.

On the Saturday before Christmas John met Marshall McLuhan in his office at the University of Toronto's Department of Culture and Technology. The meeting had been arranged by CBS Television and the cameras were filming from the moment we arrived. For forty-five minutes the silver-haired McLuhan asked John and Yoko questions and expounded his own theories on music, language, and peace. "Language is

John in his winter outfit gets ready to race through the snow in the Hawkins' Amphicat.

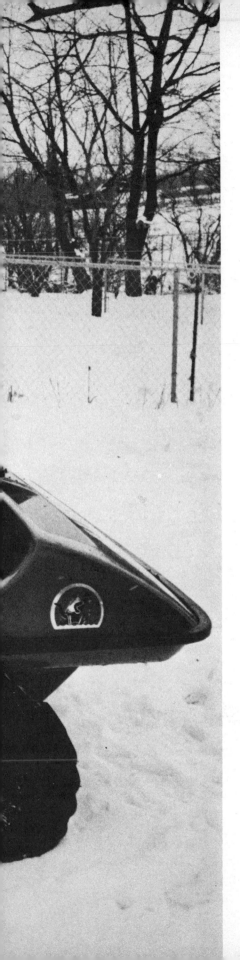

a form of organized stutter," he said. "Literally, you chop your sounds up into bits in order to talk. Now when you sing, you don't stutter, so singing is a way of stretching language into long, harmonious patterns and cycles. How do you think about language in songs?"

"Language and song is to me, apart from being pure vibrations, just like trying to describe a dream," John replied. "And because we don't have telepathy or whatever it is, we try and describe the dream to each other, to verify to each other what we know, what we believe is inside each other. And the stuttering is right—because we can't say it. No matter how you say it, it's never how you want to say it." It was a positive, intense meeting. As John and Yoko climbed into their Rolls for the drive back to the farm, McLuhan waved goodbye and said, "These portals have been honored by your presence."

Excitement built up during the week as positive signals began coming in from Ottawa regarding the meeting with Trudeau. Behind the scenes negotiations were well under way. John's representatives were meeting secretly with members of the Prime Minister's Central Office. Finally on the weekend word came through that the meeting was definitely scheduled but on condition that there be no advance publicity of any kind. The press would not be notified by the Prime Minister until the last minute. John and Yoko were excited but nervous.

The train trip to the capital began early Monday morning from Union Station. A glass-roofed observation carriage, complete with dining facilities and sleeping couchettes, had been hired for the journey. John and Yoko were in high spirits, joking constantly with Ritchie and myself. Five hours later we arrived in Montreal, where two limousines waited to rush us to the Chateau Champlain Hotel for a press conference. Back at the train, a hole was drilled in the side of our carriage and a telephone installed. John talked to London from his train seat and conducted several more peace interviews. Later that evening a secret meeting was set up at the rear of Platform 18 for John and Yoko to talk to members of Le Dain Drug Commission, which was investigating the legalization of marijuana in Canada. The discussions continued until 2:00 A.M. Tuesday when our carriage was finally hauled into Ottawa, where it was ten below zero.

We were all up half the night making various telephone calls as the tension built up. John was so nervous he couldn't sleep, but by morning he had calmed down and was feeling much more confident, resplendent in his best Cardin suit, wide black silk tie and swirling cape. At 10:30 in the morning the press were told of the Lennons' impending meeting with Prime Minister Trudeau, and at precisely 10:55 we were rushed by limousine to the Parliament buildings. Over fifty excited photographers

The glass-roofed train taking John and Yoko on their historic trip from Toronto to Ottawa to meet Prime Minister Pierre Trudeau. Left to right: John, Yoko, Anthony Fawcett, John Brower, Wanda and Ronnie Hawkins, and Ritchie Yorke.

Upper right: John and Yoko with Pierre Trudeau in his oak-paneled office at the start of their fifty-two-minute meeting.

were waiting and we had literally to fight our way up the steps as government aides escorted John and Yoko inside. After a final briefing and an exchange of pleasantries with the aides we were shown into Trudeau's oak-paneled office. He immediately suggested a quick photo session to keep the press happy. As the photographers gathered around eagerly, Trudeau said, "Well, I suppose you'd like a handshake," and he reached out to grab John's hand. Then he put his arm around Yoko and gave her a big hug. Everybody was all smiles and the press loved it; they were ushered out, the heavy oak doors closed, and the meeting began.

Both the Lennons and Trudeau were noticeably nervous as the talk began but after a few minutes the conversation warmed up. To break the ice Trudeau questioned John about his books and poetry, which he said he enjoyed. The talk turned to music, the generation gap and the state of youth, and quickly to the peace endeavors. John enthusiastically outlined the plans for the Mosport Park peace festival, explaining why he felt Canada was the best place for such an event. Trudeau seemed genuinely interested in the idea and even went so far as to offer official government endorsement and assistance.

Talking softly, the Prime Minister expounded on his trip to China and went on to ask John whether he had any private life as a Beatle. He appeared suitably impressed with John's rhetoric and the peace campaign in general. As we got up to leave Trudeau told John and Yoko that he had enjoyed meeting them and that he hoped there would be more such meetings on less formal grounds. They had given him, he said, very positive feelings about the future of youth and the part they could play in bringing peace to the world. Trudeau, for his part, was ready to give all the help he could.

Afterwards John and Yoko were besieged by the press. John, smiling and triumphant, spoke into a field of microphones: "If there were more leaders like Mr. Trudeau, the world would have peace. . . . You don't know how lucky you are in Canada." "It was a beautiful meeting," Yoko added. "We got a good incentive."

From the Prime Minister's office the Lennons were escorted to the Ministry of Health for a lengthy meeting with John Munro, the Health Minister, and senior members of his department. This was an open meeting with the press in attendance. The drug issue arose once more and the Health Department people made it clear that they didn't want the problem covered up. John was direct and honest in his defense of soft drugs, and clear in his condemnation of hard stuff. Munro asked John for his advice on the generation gap: "Often, when I talk with young people," he said, "I can't even get to open my mouth before I'm battered with placards

John and Yoko leave the Ministry of Health in Ottawa after a lengthy meeting with Health Minister John Munro.

and posters and catch phrases." "Get your own posters and fire them back," John told him.

Thus ended one of the most memorable days of John and Yoko's peace campaign, including twenty-four hours of unprecedented conferences with politicians and a rare meeting between a Prime Minister and a popular entertainer. What had been achieved was direct *communication* with the Establishment, and this is what was important to John. As we boarded the plane back to England John told reporters: "Trudeau was interested in us because he thought we might represent some sort of youth faction. We spent about fifty minutes together, which was longer than he had ever spent with any head of state, which was the great glory of the time." And back in London John told me: "It was the best trip we've ever had. We got more done for peace this week than in our whole lives."

In early January, after resting at Tittenhurst for a few days, John and Yoko left for Denmark, anxious to see Kyoko and to talk to Tony Cox about the possibility of her living with them at Ascot for a time. Yoko had really been worrying about her daughter and missing her a lot.

The Peace Festival gathered momentum in Canada. Over four hundred radio stations from the United States joined the Peace Network, which in effect was just a channel to put out Festival news. *Billboard* even donated a page to announce: "Free Peace Messages from John and Yoko Lennon, along with taped station I.D.s," and a list of all the participating stations. Everyone began talking about the Festival and estimated attendance figures of one to two million were thrown around. It was taken for granted that John would bring the other Beatles to perform, and word was out that both Dylan and Elvis would also be appearing. The Festival organizers, calling themselves Karma Productions, set up a lavish office, and a string of hip businessmen, seeing the chance for exploitation, moved in like greased lightning.

At this point the Toronto Peace Festival, or the John Lennon Peace Festival as it was being called in some circles, was still a pipe dream; it had not yet been clearly established just what John's role really was to be. To clarify this, and to show John the newly drawn up plans for the Festival site, John Brower and Ritchie Yorke left Toronto in mid-January and flew to Denmark. I drove with them through the snow-covered countryside to the farmhouse where John and Yoko were staying. After telling everybody to empty their pockets of any cigarettes or dope, Tony Cox led us through the back door. Seated around a kitchen table were John and Yoko, Allen Klein and Melinda. Their heads had been shaved and they looked terrible. It was a shock. John laughed as he said hello, and asked, "Well, what do you think?" Yoko seemed more selfconscious and tried hard to smile but she couldn't. Kyoko pulled at Brower's jacket and whispered: "I'm a girl, I'm a girl."

Talk turned immediately to the Peace Festival. John flipped through the plans and proposals and became visibly annoyed when he got to the part about the ticket price structure. "No! No! No!" he shouted, pulling out a piece of paper which he shoved in front of Brower. It read: "Free (for one dollar) John Lennon Peace Festival. Toronto, July 3, 4, 5, to celebrate the year 1 A.P. War is over if you want it."

Brower and Yorke couldn't believe it. How could you have a "free" festival, they argued, with the enormous costs of food, sanitation, and other necessary amenities. It was impossible. But John was stubborn, the free festival was the only kind of festival he'd have anything to do with. He then added that they should return to Toronto, draw up new plans and submit them to him by March 1 for his approval. He also informed them that Hammrick and Leonard (two "Harbinger" friends of Cox who had come to exert a strange influence over John) would help to coordinate everything, and that they would act as liaisons. Klein interrupted to say that he would be involved in the business side, signing groups and setting up the Peace Foundation.

John Brower and Ritchie Yorke left Denmark sad and disillusioned, knowing that a Free Festival could not work. John had completely gone back on what he had said in public, only a month before. Announcing the Peace Festival in Toronto a few days prior to his meeting with Trudeau, John had said:

"We want to set up something that people will get wages and money for. Otherwise it's another charity affair, so they will get paid. I think there's enough money to be made out of a show like this for everyone."

The last straw came a month later when Leonard and the other Harbingers called a press conference in San Francisco to announce that flying saucers would be landing at the event. They also revealed plans for their "air-car," a two-passenger car that looked like a plane and which could go on the ground or fly in the air. More importantly, they added, it never needed fuel, as it was powered by psychic energy. And one was being built for John and Yoko to use for their arrival at the Festival. Trudeau was reported to be "not amused."

Brower tried to ignore the worst, and made one last vain attempt to send John plans for an organized professional festival. Yorke, who had been traveling around the world to promote John and Yoko's peace message, resigned. Back in London, John came to his senses and realized that the "space-ship" people had gone too far. But he was still adamant about a *free* festival and decided that it was time to pull out. He gave me a telegram to send to Brower in Toronto: "Just read your report. You have done exactly what we told you not to. We said it was to be free. We want nothing to do with you or your festival. Please do not use our name or our ideas or symbols. John and Yoko Lennon."

It all happened so fast. Afterwards John was sad and disillusioned. He had given his name and his trust to a few too many people, and of course this backfired. With the Peace Festival aborted he and Yoko sank back into self-involvement. For them the peace trip, as a way of life, was over.

Overall, John and Yoko's peace campaign was effective; their message certainly reached the youth of the world, although John's most important personal contribution was probably "Give Peace A Chance," which united thousands at the Moratoriums in America.

John and Yoko shared the dream of a united world, beyond nationalism. They realized that the first step toward peace is to promote understanding among nations by viewing all men from a single perspective. Reflecting on the events of the peace crusade, John said at the end of 1969: "I know that some of what we have done together has looked silly. But I don't regret any of it. Why should I? We did it after all. I know that a lot of what I say is repetitious and ordinary. But what we have to say is really very simple. We are not ashamed of its simplicity. We're just determined to go on saying it until someone does something about it. And you try and answer ten million interviews a day and try and think of something different to say each time . . .

"Some people discovered a new reality and some people are still confident about the future, like we two are. Everybody's talking about the way it's going, the decadence and the rest of it, but not many people are noticing all the good that came out of the last ten years, which is the Moratorium, the vast gathering of people in Woodstock, which is the biggest mass of people ever gathered together for anything other than the war."

Certainly people became more socially conscious during the sixties and there is now more serious analysis than before. Also, as much as John was trying to influence youth, he was at the same time a reflection of the generation that battled for peace with buttons and bumper stickers, posters and slogans, picket lines and petitions, sit-ins and antiwar protests.

Even from the perspective of the midseventies, John does not feel that his energies were wasted: "I am not in the group of people who think that because all our dreams didn't come true in the Sixties everything we said or did was invalid. No, there isn't any peace in the world despite our efforts, but I still believe the hippie peace-and-love thing was worthwhile. If somebody stands up and smiles and then gets smacked in the face, that doesn't invalidate the smile. It existed." John's feeling about peace is the same today as it was then, and can be summed up, simply, by the words of Bradford Smith:

"There is a politic beyond politics
Which is concerned with the freedom
of man's mind and spirit.
It looks beyond communism or capitalism
to the welfare of the human family."

MONOPOLY AT APPLE AND THE MISSISSIPPI GAMBLER

"He plays it by ear [Allen Klein] doesn't he! Some people play different . . . they're all playing chess you know . . . To me he's bluffing his way through—he's a gambler, like one of those Mississippi gamblers, and if he's on a lucky streak we'll make it through, and if he's not on a lucky streak we've fucking had it!"   (John Lennon, 1969)

On my first visit to Apple I had walked slowly upstairs over the thick green carpet, trying to take in everything frame by frame, savoring the feeling of the place and the electric energy in the air. The mere presence of the Beatles had endowed the building with a feeling of "Wonderland," and I felt a "through the looking-glass" sensation upon entering Number Three Savile Row. The whitewashed Georgian townhouse, complete with flagpole, looked more like a royal embassy than a record company headquarters—except that a swarm of young girls, "Apple scruffs," were camped out on the steps.

In April 1969, Yoko had called a meeting to discuss the possibility of my working full time for her and John, rather than just helping them with art projects. They were ensconced in green velvet armchairs—the kind you sink into—in Peter Brown's spacious office, an interior decorator's dream combination of cool Italian furniture carefully arranged within a room of rich Georgian proportions. While an office boy piled logs onto the fire in the ornate carved wood fireplace John sat staring into space, pulling gently at the beard he had recently grown. Yoko jumped up to greet me and asked me to sit on the floor next to them.

Without a word of explanation John turned suddenly, looked me square in the face and barked: "Right, well here's what we're doing then," and proceeded to reel off twenty or thirty ideas and projects as well as what action should be taken on each, while I tried frantically to write it all down. Presumably I had the job, but I didn't have time to ask; my brain was deluged with thoughts and sensations. John and Yoko were such an amalgam of eccentricities—part genius, part egomaniac, part clown— that the thought of working for them and being intimately involved in their lives elated me. It wasn't just the thrill of who they were, or their life-style, it was the challenge of entering the unknown, the bizarre, where one never knew what to expect next. Just be ready for the unexpected, I told myself.

John's nasal voice interrupted my train of thought: "Well now we have an assistant we'll need our own office, right?" Yoko nodded her agreement, and John jumped up out of his chair to confront Peter Brown. "Which is the best office in the building?" he asked.

Perhaps afraid of losing his own extravaganza, Brown replied nervously: "Oh, er, Ron Kass's office downstairs is one of the biggest, and it looks out onto Savile Row. And actually Ron is away on vacation right now."

"Right," John said. "Let's go," and he led the way downstairs. After bursting into a large high-ceilinged room he glanced around, seemed satisfied, and then asked the startled secretaries to pack everything up and leave—this was now to be his office, he explained. Five minutes later John and Yoko were sitting behind an oversize chrome and leather desk and I was almost lost on the other side of the room, behind two futuristic white desks and a frightening array of telephones.

When we first took it over, the office was cool, impersonal and all-white—white Italian furniture, white filing cabinets, a built-in white stereo console and a white television. The only color came from a green carpet and the dark leather of a corner couch. Within a matter of days John and Yoko had changed the feeling of the room entirely. The walls were covered with framed photographs and posters of the couple, along with several of John's cartoons. The office became an elegant, ever changing John and Yoko exhibition. Although the whiteness remained it was only to create a perfect background for their many projects.

On April 22, 1969, shortly after I began to work for them, John changed his middle name from Winston to Ono, in honor of Yoko, in an official ceremony on the roof of Apple. Both dressed in black leather outfits, silhouetted against the West-End skyline with their long hair blowing in the wind, John and Yoko laughed, kissed and strutted around as the Commissioner for Oaths performed the ceremony. Photographer David Nutter clicked away, capturing the scene on film. After the event John, who was now legally John Ono Lennon, said: "Yoko changed hers for me, I've changed mine for her. One for both, both for each other. She has a ring. I have a ring. It gives us nine 'O's' between us, which is good luck. Ten would not be good luck. Three names is enough for anyone. Four would be greedy."

I set about organizing the office. We received an avalanche of mail and

On the roof of Apple, John changed his middle name from Winston to Ono, in an official ceremony performed by the Commissioner of Oaths. Opposite page: After the ceremony John and Yoko pose against the London skyline.

John and Yoko's office at Apple—on the ground floor
and looking out onto Savile Row. Almost every day they sat
behind their black leather desk and gave ten to fifteen interviews,
sustained by hot tea and macrobiotic food. The walls
became an ever-changing John and Yoko exhibition, covered
with cartoons, photos, and posters.

press clippings daily, hundreds of letters asking John to appear at benefits, and of course the continual requests for press interviews. John and Yoko drove in from the country most days and usually arrived at the office around lunchtime. They immediately pored over every memo, piece of mail, and press clipping, while they ate a macrobiotic dish of brown rice and vegetables smothered in tamari sauce. We would discuss the projects arranged for the day and I would fill them in on the interviews that had been set up—usually ten or twelve every day—to promote their peace ideas, or talk about new records or films.

John enjoyed having his own office and was happy even when the interviews were long and grueling and left him exhausted at the end of the day. A fresh pot of tea always revived him. He was concerned and involved in what was going on in the rest of the building. He always wanted to hear acetates and mixes of all the records going out on the new Apple label, and he watched the sales figures closely.

I found myself totally immersed in the intricacies of John's life and my responsibility doubled when both John and Yoko began to rely on me as a personal computer. Late at night, after everybody had gone home, the fire would still be burning in our office; there would always be countless proposals to be documented and memos to be readied for their arrival the next day, when the crazy pace would begin again. Sergeant Swain, the night security guard who had become so much a part of the building, would stick his head in periodically to utter a friendly word or cull some new piece of gossip. The telephones rang incessantly far into the night; most of the calls were from young American girls crying and begging to find out whether it was really true about Paul being dead. The Sergeant consoled them all.

During my first weeks of working for John and Yoko it was the little things that surprised me, like the amount of mail they got every day and the care taken to read it all, and to reply to many of the letters; and their accessibility. It seemed as if anyone who either wrote a good enough letter to interest John, or waited in Apple's reception area long enough, could eventually come in and have a meeting with him.

I soon noticed that John had a special sort of power. He didn't have to exert himself to use it, it just seemed to flow from him. His personality was electric, his wit razor sharp, and his whole being radiated an alertness I had never seen before. Another of John's most noticeable characteristics was his seemingly inexhaustible supply of energy. It seemed as if he were driven by some powerful inner dynamo that constantly recharged itself. Whatever he did and wherever he went his waves of energy would splash around engulfing everyone in close proximity.

At the EMI Studios in Abbey Road John and Yoko
work on a new song together.

John and Yoko's closeness to each other was always evident and often touching. Yoko never left John's side and even during interviews she would cuddle up next to him behind their desk in the office. It was as if they each needed constant reassurance that the other one was still there.

Apple was energized by John's daily presence in the building; you could feel excitement and tension in the air the minute he walked through the door. Once in the office he was in the habit of buzzing different departments via the intercom to check what was happening. He liked to keep everyone on their toes. George and Ringo appeared every three or four days but Paul had gotten bored and had stopped coming into Apple regularly. John was the only one you could count on to be in for long periods every day. "I am at 3 Savile Row, most days," read the bottom of one unusually intense press photo of John put out by the inimitable Derek Taylor.

Apple was conceived in 1967. After their disappointment with the *Magical Mystery Tour* film the Beatles had decided to combine their business affairs into some sort of coherent whole. While at the Maharishi's retreat they formulated the general idea.

"We wanted to help other people," said John, "but without it being like charity and without seeming like patrons of the arts. *We* always had to go to the big man on our knees, touch our forelocks and say: 'please, Mr. Man, can we do so and so?' And most of the big companies are so big and so out of touch with people like us, who just want to sing or make films, that everybody has a bad time. We were just trying to set up a good organization, not some great fat institution that doesn't care. We didn't want people to say yessir and nosir. We were in the happy position of not needing any more money, so we hoped that for the first time the bosses wouldn't be in it for the money. If you had come to me and said: 'I've had such-and-such a dream, I probably would have said 'here's so much money, go away and do it.' We'd already bought all *our* dreams. All we wanted was to share that possibility with others."

John and Paul held the first American board meeting of Apple in May 1968, aboard a hired Chinese junk which sailed, appropriately, around the Statue of Liberty in New York harbor. Liberty was precisely what they aimed to achieve in their new organization, liberty not only to manage their affairs but also to offer others certain opportunities they felt had been closed to them.

The legal and financial structure of Apple Corps was conceived by their then chief financial advisor Harold Pinsker, a senior partner in one of

London's leading show-business accounting firms. But their first flirtation with retailing, through clothes shops on London's Baker Street and Kings Road, convinced them that their tax problems would be solved more readily if they went into films, electronic inventions and record production. The first record they released on their new label, also called Apple, confirmed this: "Hey Jude" eventually outsold and outgrossed every other single record they had ever made.

When Apple was founded Paul said it was to be a "cheerful, energetic and democratic commercial adventure which will eventually lead to the establishment of a Foundation to benefit neglected charities." There was also to be an "Apple Foundation of the Arts, for the encouragement of unknown talents." Barely eighteen months later he was unhappy about the combined "unknown talent" of John and Yoko, and was already disillusioned about Apple itself, writing for the last Beatle album ["Abbey Road"]: "You never give me your money/You only give me funny paper/And in the middle of negotiations/You break down . . ." in direct reference to the mounting financial difficulties of the company.

Desperate to put Apple in some kind of order the Beatles considered hiring several leading British business executives but none of them seemed suitable, or even felt that they could solve the problem. As John explained: "The problem is that two years ago our accountants made us sign over 80 percent of all our royalties to Apple. All the money comes into this little building and it never gets out. If I could get my money out of the company, I'd split away and start doing my own projects independently. I'd have much more freedom and we'd all be happier."

In addition to the monetary problems John was also feeling hurt and rejected by the abuse that Yoko had been receiving from the Apple staff in general, and even from his fellow Beatles. "I still feel part of Apple and the Beatles," he said, "and there's no animosity, but they tend to ignore Yoko and me. For instance Kenny Everett, a British disc jockey, recently made a promotional record for Apple which was played at the big yearly E.M.I. meeting. It plugged James Taylor, the Ivies, and so on, but it didn't mention the things Yoko and I have been doing. And I think that what we're doing is a lot more important than James Taylor; Apple seems to be scared of us."

John's feelings of isolation and rejection by his own company were exacerbated by the conflict over Allen Klein, an American business manager who for several years had been successfully handling the Rolling Stones. John's statement early in 1969 that "if Apple goes on losing money all of us will be broke within six months," precipitated Klein's arrival.

"We didn't have anything in the bank really, none of us did," John complained. "Paul and I could probably have floated it, but we were sinking fast. It was just hell and it had to stop. When Allen [Klein] heard me say that—he read it in *Rolling Stone*—he came over right away."

Some hint of the truth came from Steve Maltz, a young accountant at Apple, who sent John a letter saying: "You're in chaos, you're losing money, there is so much a week going out of Apple."

"People were robbing us and living on us," John said bitterly. "Eighteen or twenty thousand pounds a week was rolling out of Apple and nobody was doing anything about it. All our buddies that worked for us for fifty years were all just living and drinking and eating like fuckin' Rome, and I suddenly realised it . . . we're losing money at such a rate that we would have been broke, really broke."

John decided he had better do something. "I tried at first to assess the situation myself," he said. "But I'd keep losing the initiative. I'd get fed up because I could never quite get the full picture." He desperately needed to find somebody who *could* find out the full picture and who would be firm, and that somebody turned out to be Allen Klein. It was really out of despair that John agreed finally to meet with him; Klein had been suggesting a meeting for some time. Already having the Stones, it was no secret in the business that Klein's dream was to have the Beatles as well. The public and private rebuff John had endured as a result of the "Two Virgins" record finally pushed him into it: "I knew of him through Mick Jagger and the Rolling Stones. He had been looking after them quite well, so I trusted him—as much as I trusted any business man, that is."

Allen Klein was tough, a true wheeler-dealer, but as a person he was warm and likable. John liked Allen because he was so human and a self-made man like himself. Also, the fact that Klein had been an orphan, like John's father, touched a soft spot. They got on very well together and found they had a lot in common.

Their first meeting was at the Dorchester Hotel and it was a traumatic experience for John because he was nervous. When he saw that Klein, too, was nervous, he felt better, and they talked for hours about each other's backgrounds. John was amazed that Klein knew so much about his music—even the lyrics he had written years before. Later that night John and Yoko decided that Klein was their man and John immediately sent off a letter to the head of E.M.I., Sir Joe Lockwood, telling him of Klein's appointment to look after his personal financial affairs.

John's next step was to tell Paul, George and Ringo his decision and

In the Apple offices the Beatles sign a contract with American businessman Allen Klein, the man John thought of as a "Mississippi Gambler." Pictured left to right: Yoko, John, Klein, Paul, and Ringo.

bring them around to his way of thinking. Previously, Paul had asked John to go and see several of Britain's leading business consultants, including Lord Beeching, in order to find the right person to run Apple. John, however, was disappointed in all of them, and felt that none was right for the job.

Paul McCartney, who since Epstein's death had virtually taken it upon himself to "lead" the Beatles and make all the important decisions, had different ideas. He wanted his father-in-law, Lee Eastman, a New York music business lawyer, to manage Apple and the Beatles' affairs. In fact it had been a near thing; before meeting Klein, John had been introduced to John Eastman, Lee's son. With no alternative at that time Lennon had almost agreed to sign.

When Allen Klein first came on the scene the Eastmans panicked. John was still open to the possibility of using them, and a meeting was set up to hold discussions with the Eastmans, Klein, and all four Beatles. The meeting had barely begun when Lee Eastman became almost hysterical, screaming insults at Allen Klein and calling him all sorts of names. Klein calmly sat there and took it. Eastman's class snobbery and resentment of Klein turned John off immediately, and he decided right away that he would never let a man like that handle him.

The inability of Klein and Eastman to come to terms with each other created two totally opposed, hostile camps. Klein was in, as far as John Lennon was concerned, and it didn't take him long to persuade George and Ringo. Klein was convincing because he said that he would only take twenty percent of *increased* Beatle business. If things stayed as they were he wouldn't get a penny. Even though Paul at first refused to sign any contract with him, Klein still had the majority support and he proceeded as if he had all four Beatles signed up. The idea was for Klein to make enough money to please the Beatles or he would go; the papers signed constituted a three-year bond, but either party could cancel at the end of each year.

Klein was fast, a bundle of energy, his tubby body trying hard to synchronize with his lightning mind. His face was open and youthful, his eyes alert, and when he talked to you about money or business they would twinkle, shining with some sort of inward pleasure. Klein was everywhere. He would often turn up late at night at the Beatles' recording sessions at Abbey Road. He tried to pry information out of you as if you were a can of sardines. He would walk down the long corridors with me, put his arm around my shoulder, and ask me what John was *really* thinking about something.

I never found Klein frightening, as so many people did, even Apple insiders. The Apple staff appeared to resent him—understandably, as he was after all a threat to their existence—and many of them chose to leave rather than be kicked out.

After Klein had been at work for a few months John was a little happier because he could at least understand what was going on, and was more aware of their earlier mistakes:

"I realised that we had wasted many of our investments. Northern Songs, for example. We were happy to leave it alone. We presumed that it was ticking over quite nicely, thank you, getting hits as we were all the time. Now I began to realise that more could have been done. For the first time I got to know where all the money comes from, where it goes, where it went, and where it's gonna come from. Now I wouldn't sign anything until someone explains to me what every clause in small print means. Now that I know what a merchant banker is I won't hesitate to go to one in the future for backing. But he won't be 'handling me,' which was always what happened in the past. A merchant banker is like a tailor, and a tailor doesn't tell you what to wear. Money isn't a dirty word for me anymore, although I'm still not particularly interested in securities or shares. After all I am a share."

Bag Productions had been set up during the summer to handle John and Yoko's ever increasing film catalog and any other projects or merchandising ideas they came up with. "Before I was famous I used to cadge money off people. But I always knew at the back of my mind that I'd finish up well off. I think I always wanted to be an eccentric millionaire—and I am. My only regret is that we originally set up Apple in an attempt to get away from all the big business men giving us orders. Now we've finished up worse than we were before, and poorer. I've even had to set up my own company with Yoko—Bag Productions—to keep some of the pennies from going down the Apple drain."

Autumn of 1969 was chaotic in Apple, not only for the number of business crises going down but also for the "Paul is dead" rumor that was sweeping America, and the filmmaking marathons of John and Yoko.

The rumor about Paul's death had sprung from "clues" apparently to be found on the front cover of the Beatles' "Abbey Road" album. Paul, or his stand-in as the story hypothesized, was the only Beatle out of step and the only one barefoot. The Apple switchboard was being inundated with calls from girls all over the United States who wanted to know if it was true.

The day of the album cover photo session Paul was very much alive. I arrived late and when I got to the E.M.I. Studios John asked me to help the photographer, Iain McMillan, with anything he needed. Everybody was laughing about the fact that Paul had arrived with no shoes, and even though his house was just around the corner he said he couldn't be bothered to go get any. McMillan set up his camera in the middle of Abbey Road, right outside the studios, and while the police stopped traffic the Beatles walked across the road three or four times. He kept shouting: "Stop! Start again," until he was confident that he had the right shot.

Happy with the front cover, McMillan asked me to drive with him along Abbey Road to look for the best street sign to photograph for the back cover. It had to be one of the old-style tiled signs set into the bricks. The best one was at the far end of Abbey Road and we set up the camera on the edge of the pavement. McMillan decided to take a series of shots and was angry when, in the middle of them, a girl in a blue dress walked by, oblivious to what was happening. But this turned out to be the most interesting shot and the Beatles chose it for the back cover. Afterwards I joined John and Yoko at Paul's house in St. John's Wood, where everybody had gone for tea after the photo session.

Two weeks later, on September 10, 1969, the first of two evenings of John and Yoko's films was presented at the Institute of Contemporary Arts (ICA). Filmmaking had become something of a passion for John and Yoko; they had devoted hundreds of hours to filming, editing and re-editing. It was a creative experience they could share, it was fun, and it took their minds off more depressing problems.

The first program was made up of two films, the British premiere of *Rape* and the world premiere of *Self Portrait. Rape* had been made for Austrian television, where it was first shown on March 31, 1969. The film dealt with the pursuit of a young girl by an overly aggressive camera crew. The girl, a twenty-one-year-old Hungarian refugee named Eva Majlata, had no idea of the purpose or plot of the film, in which she is "raped by camera." The idea behind the film was to show the effect that the relentlessly news-hungry media can have on public personalities such as John and Yoko. Ironically this was the first of their films to receive favorable reviews from the press.

When *Rape* had its world premiere in Vienna, John and Yoko appeared at the press conference, in the famous Red Salon of the Sacher Hotel, inside a large white bag. This "bagism," as they called it, was derived from one of Yoko's earlier art events, and was a way of promoting "total communication," because whoever was inside the bag could speak

"Stop! Start again!" shouted photographer Iain McMillan until he was confident he had the right shot of the Beatles crossing Abbey Road. Later we looked for the best old-style street sign for the back cover (bottom).

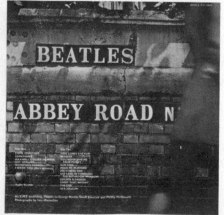

freely and not feel prejudiced against by his or her looks.

Self Portrait was an indulgent Warholian piece of film which consisted of a fifteen-minute slow motion shot of John Lennon's erection. Presumably this excursion into the ridiculous was a product of John's humor and his sense of the absurd, and part of his game of baiting the critics. When questioned about being a leader around this time, John had told a reporter: "So I refuse to lead, and I'll always show my genitals or something which prevents me from being Martin Luther King or Gandhi, and getting killed."

John and Yoko had promised to attend the ICA's film show; however, when the day arrived they decided not to go themselves but instead to send their "bag." So we set about finding a substitute couple who were about the right size, and eventually chose two friends of an Apple secretary. After they had been briefed and had put on the bag I led them to John's white Rolls. The chauffeur drove us to the Institute, where I helped the "bag" out of the car as flash bulbs popped and TV crews filmed what they thought was John and Yoko's entrance. I led the "bag" down the theater aisle and up onto the stage, where as arranged they sat down beside the screen. During the performance the audience was encouraged to participate by four blonde hostesses who handed out wooden spoons and biscuit tins to bang on. The couple inside the bag rang bells and wailed a *Hare Krishna* style chant. One critic later said he recognized John's nasal voice. As a final gesture John and Yoko also arranged for their film crew to creep around the auditorium filming the critics' reactions to each film, using special infra-red stock.

Enjoying the role of "film director," John put all his energy into making *Apotheosis,* which was their first attempt at a wide-screen, feature-length color movie. As always, the plan of the film was vague at the beginning, but included using a hot-air balloon. John and Yoko hoped to attach a camera to the balloon basket to capture the feeling of floating up through the clouds and breaking through into the clear sky.

After a balloonist was found who was willing to cooperate and cameraman Nick Knowland had been persuaded to go up with the balloon, we all assembled early one foggy September morning at a deserted airfield near Basingstoke. The first problem was to construct a solid wooden platform on the basket that would hold the heavy 35mm camera securely in place. Next John decided that he wanted a slow-motion shot of himself and Yoko, starting at their feet, then panning up their bodies over their heads, and on up into the sky. It was a difficult shot that had to be taken directly from the balloon as it started its ascent. Several times the wind almost blew the balloon out of control, and everybody had to fling themselves onto the side of the basket to keep it from dragging across the ground. Finally a successful shot was "in the can" and the balloon lifted slowly into the clouds.

When we looked at the rushes a few days later at Tatooist International, the film crew's headquarters in Soho, John decided that the balloon sequences hadn't captured the feeling he wanted of breaking through the clouds, because the balloon hadn't been able to climb high enough. His new plan was to hire a helicopter and send Nick Knowland back into the sky to film cloud formations and the vast open skies. The resulting thousands of feet of film were then edited by John and Yoko into a workable film. The title *Apotheosis* was suggested by a friend, Derek Hill, the Film Organizer of the ICA, where the film was premiered at the second John and Yoko film night, in early October 1969.

The saga of *Apotheosis* was not over. Still not happy with the balloon sequence, John made plans to reshoot it in the village square of Lavenham, Sussex, England's best preserved Tudor village. There was snow on the ground when we arrived and three cameras were set up on different sides of the square. By the time the big orange balloon was ready to lift off it was almost dusk. A fire was built to heat up the helium, and the glow lit up the black-caped figures of John and Yoko hovering around the balloon. All this footage turned out to be very beautiful and was used in *Apotheosis No. 2.*

Allen Klein always talked about the fantastic film deals he could make for John and Yoko. This excited Yoko; she would have loved to see their films shown all over America, and Klein made it sound so possible. They also tried to get him to put up some of his own companies' money to float their own Bag Productions. But Klein just carried on talking in circles. John was beginning to have his doubts about Klein, who had promised many things besides selling their films for large amounts of money. In fact, Klein had failed in his first two major projects, to get control of Northern Songs and to buy back Epstein's former company, Nems, from Triumph Investments.

Klein had vowed he would regain control of Northern Songs, which had been founded in 1963 to handle the songwriting business of Lennon and McCartney. Two weeks after John and Yoko were married a fight had begun over control of Northern and suddenly every big corporation, every merchant banker, stockbroker and wheeler-dealer in London was rushing to get a piece of the Beatle action. When all this began, John had said: "I'm enjoying it all very much, it's just like monopoly," an attitude that he quickly reversed.

Klein tried to keep Northern out of the hands of England's Associated Television (ATV), but when a consortium of financial companies added its fourteen percent to ATV's holdings, the Beatles lost the battle. The next problem was whether to sell their own stock and have nothing to do with ATV, or whether to share in the profits. After all, Northern's major assets were over seventy Lennon and McCartney songs and John and Paul owned about thirty-one percent of the stock. They finally decided to sell out, and it was announced in October that they were selling to ATV for $4.8 million.

With the Northern defeat Klein really had to set about justifying his presence to John, who was under constant pressure from Paul. At the time it was difficult to understand how anyone could have cut himself in for twenty percent of the Beatles' earnings. The press did not go along with John's reasoning and came out very heavily against Klein. He was considered a bizarre choice for the Beatles, who had a long established record of honesty in their business dealings. Epstein may have been tough across the bargaining table but his integrity was widely respected. To *Rolling Stone* it "defied imagination that John Lennon, whose anti-bullshit stance—with his peace crusade, his uncompromising demand for honesty from his fellow man—should have connected the Beatles with such a man, at a time when they had a real opportunity to define a whole new style of conducting the business affairs of the media and the entertainment industry. We have come to expect innovation, new perspectives, and honesty, above all, honesty—from the Beatles, and especially John."

Klein himself said later in a rare interview: "The Beatles were almost broke and didn't even have control over their own songs, or even their records. So I was trying to free them; get their past back for them and free the future. I wanted to get John and Paul their songs back or else to just get rid of their involvement in Northern altogether."

Proving himself to John was now Klein's main incentive and he set about negotiating a new contract for the Beatles with E.M.I. Their exclusive recording contract was due to expire in 1976 but they had fulfilled the minimum requirements of five LPs and five singles by 1969, so Klein was in a great bargaining position to demand more cash for future records. Klein's tough argument to E.M.I. was "no increased royalty, no more records." The result was impressive; the renegotiated terms gave the Beatles twenty-five percent of the wholesale price from American sales, an unusually large cut. The increased royalties were subject to the Beatles fulfilling a minimum provision of two LPs a year until 1976, either collectively or individually. E.M.I. executives admitted that "few people could have beaten out such a good contract," and "although he is confusing to negotiate with he's a very good businessman."

Klein said: "These were not easy deals to put together; the financial tangles the Beatles were in were incredible. I was there working my ass off to get them what they deserved."

The contract marked a turning point in the relationship between Klein and John. Klein had proved himself to all of them except Paul, even though Paul was happy to sign the E.M.I. contract after Klein's hard work. Apple's problems were still far from solved, however, and discussions were begun about the possibility of selling it. George Harrison said candidly: "It's really like Vietnam, the way I see it, it's escalated. It's got so big, but we can't really see the way out."

It was ironic that even though John and Paul often agreed about what had to be done, their separate advisors, Klein and Eastman, could not bring themselves to agree or even to try working together for the Beatles' common good. Klein and Eastman's inability to come to terms with each other inevitably widened the split between John and Paul, who tried desperately to hammer out their differences and come to joint decisions.

Paul would say to John: "The four of us aren't going to cheat each other, and the four of us are going to remain together in the one objective—of *somehow* getting it so we can get the money out of Apple. Then, rather than actually work out the plan ourselves, which we couldn't really do, have a meeting with them and say: 'the four of us want *this,*' and I'm not now speaking as Eastman's client, and you're not speaking as Klein's client . . . All I want is for the four of us to just agree on it, then I think we can win it. We can just get what we want."

To which John would invariably reply: "Yeah, but you see what they both say, like what happened last time—Klein'll say: 'I can't possibly work unless I have full control,' and Eastman'll say: 'I can't possibly work unless I have full control,' and then we get to that decision of who we're gonna use again!"

Paul came close at times to accepting Klein completely, but there was always that nagging doubt at the back of his mind that Klein would say one thing and then do another, and to the very end John never knew exactly what was going on—to him it really was just monopoly, even though he tried so hard to understand everything; sadly, John and Paul were really fighting for the same thing—to save Apple, right up until the eleventh hour. In the end they both gave up. The dream of Apple had long since dissolved, lost along the way among the remnants of high ideals and conceptual energy, buried beneath the accountant's nightmare and the sponger's leftovers, drifting in limbo. Finally, in December 1970, Paul began High Court proceedings to end the Beatles' partnership, a sad and desperate measure to stop Klein running Apple in cloaked secrecy and to put the company's transactions into the hands of a receiver. If the Mississippi Gambler was on a lucky streak, neither John nor Paul shared in the winning aces.

THE BREAKUP OF THE BEATLES

"The problem is we've all got these millions of songs . . . how can we fit 'em on that ten little minutes . . . This is the compromise of being the Beatles, that there's no more time for me to put 'Revolution No. 9' on Beatles albums, because that's John Lennon."   (John Lennon, 1969)

It was John's basic insecurity about his own creativity that led to Paul McCartney's gradual dominance and the resulting conflict between them. After their touring days John's actual role in the Beatles had become a passive one, contrary to his public image. He had retreated into his own world, away from the other Beatles. Then when Yoko appeared, he lost himself in her world, removing himself even further from Paul's conservative aspirations.

After Brian Epstein's death in the summer of 1967, Paul decided that *he* should keep the group going and come up with new ideas and projects. John was both stunned and scared by Brian's death and from that moment on the end of the Beatles was in sight. "After Brian died we collapsed," John said later in *Lennon Remembers*: "We broke up then. That was the disintegration. Paul made an attempt to carry on as if Brian hadn't died, by saying: 'now, now boys, we're going to make a record.'"*

The record turned into a film, the disastrous *Magical Mystery Tour,* the Beatles' first failure in the eyes of the critics and the public. As far as John was concerned the problem was that Paul had come up with a fully worked out idea with most of the music already written. John wanted to be in on the conception of the idea, or even better to be the originator himself, as in the old days. But this was impossible because he was too lost in his own world, feeling his own pain. It was a vicious circle.

Paul first thought of the idea for *Magical Mystery Tour* while on a flight home from America in April 1967. The main reason for an hour-long television film was to appease the fans, who continued to complain that the Beatles had deserted them by refusing to make any more live ap-

*Lennon Remembers: The Rolling Stone Interviews. Straight Arrow Books, San Francisco, 1971.

pearances. The film was to consist of the Beatles themselves plus a few friends, on a bus tour. It would be "magical" since they intended to film whatever came into their heads as they went along, and it would be "mysterious" in that neither they nor any of their passengers would have the faintest idea of where they were going or what they might do next.

Paul wrote out the basic outline on a scrap of paper, took it to John, and said: "well, here's a segment, you write a piece for that." Taken aback, John thought: "I've never made a film, what's he mean, write a script?" But he set to work anyway: "So I ran off and wrote the dream sequence for the fat woman and all the things with the spaghetti and all that." *

After the film's two viewings on British television at Christmas time 1967, the public reacted angrily against it and the Beatles. The daily newspapers dismissed it as "blatant rubbish." Paul was bitter about the film's failure. He felt that he had to take the blame for it because it was his idea, even though he had given the other Beatles a chance to say no. John, however, looked back on *Magical Mystery* with humor and affection. He told Paul: "I don't regret *Magical Mystery,* I think it was great—I think it'll prove that in the end; I just think that it was a good piece of work and we were fucked up by cameramen, but that's not important 'cause you probably think that it was more fucked up than I do, because you like professionalism, yer know, but I enjoyed the fish and chip quality of *Magical Mystery*—the fact that we went out with a load of freaks and tried to make a film is great, yer know!"

Magical Mystery Tour was the beginning of the end from John's point of view, not just because it hadn't been his idea, but because Paul was taking up all the time in the recording studios with his songs, and not giving John and the others their fair share on the resulting records. Paul would tell John that since he had eight or ten songs written they ought to get into the studios right away, which gave John barely a few days to come up with his work.

In September 1969, when John finally decided to leave the Beatles, he told Paul bluntly: "It was carte blanche because you'd come up with a *Magical Mystery Tour.* I didn't write any of that except 'Walrus'; I'd accept it and you'd already have five or six songs, so I'd think 'fuck it, I can't keep up with that.' So I didn't bother, yer know—and I thought I don't really care whether I was on or not, I convinced myself it didn't matter, and so for a period if you didn't invite me to be on an album *personally,* if you three didn't say: 'write some more 'cause we like your work,' I wasn't going to fight!"

John's feeling of having to fight to record his songs in the studio and to

Lennon Remembers: The Rolling Stone Interviews. Straight Arrow Books, San Francisco, 1971.

In the engineer's booth at EMI Studios Paul tries to hold things together as the Beatles listen to a playback of the live "Let It Be" sessions. John flops onto the four-track board (center) and Ringo falls asleep (below).

get them included on the Beatles' albums built up during the last three years the group was together. From *Magical Mystery Tour* on his relationship to the Beatles was a constant strain; half the problem was that he kept everything inside, increasing his own pain and getting more and more depressed. Instead of trying to tell Paul how he felt or stand up for his rights, John virtually gave up and let Paul dominate the recording sessions.

But even before this time there had been an ongoing struggle over the Beatles' singles. Paul would invariably push to get *his* song on the 'A' side. This fighting over songs and sides was finally the cause of John's decision to leave. As he told Paul: "If you look back on the Beatles' albums, good or bad or whatever you think of 'em, you'll find that most times if anybody has got extra time it's *you!* For no other reason than you worked it like that. Now when we get into a studio I don't want to go through games with you to get space on the album, yer know! I don't want to go through a little maneuvering, or whatever level it's on, to get time. 'Cause there was a time, about three years ago, I gave up fighting for an 'A' side or fighting for time. I just thought, well I'm content to put 'Walrus' on the 'B' side, when I think it's much better, and 'Strawberry Fields,' because I'm content to be on, yer know, and get the cooperation of the group to produce a 'Walrus' and a 'Strawberry Fields' out of all of you.

"I didn't have the energy or the nervous type of thing to push it, yer know. So I relaxed a bit—nobody else relaxed, you didn't relax in that way. So gradually I was submerging."

Paul, upset and a little taken aback, agreed that he had "come out stronger." But he reminded John that there had been times when he had tried hard to include John's work, only to be dismayed because he was not prepared and had written only one or two songs.

John acknowledged that he had given up writing as well as fighting, and explained: "There was no point in turning 'em out—I couldn't, didn't have the energy to turn 'em out *and* get 'em on as well."

They could talk about it forever but it was too late. John had already decided and he gave Paul his ultimatum: "When we get into the studio I don't care how we do it but I don't want to think about equal time—I just want it known I'm allowed to put four songs on the album, whatever happens! I don't have to say: 'shall we do it now?' 'cause I think we'll all get fed up in three weeks or actually the album will be full, 'cause actually we did two of Paul's last week, or one of Ringo's or one of George's, whatever, and well it's too late now—next album.

The cold, cavernous Twickenham Studios, where the Beatles filmed and recorded "Let It Be."

"I've discovered how I am, and I've got to stop it, 'cause it does me no good, yer know. I'm always bitter afterwards, and it's nobody's fault except me own. So now I'm saying no more ideas on me, or whatever, no more finished product. I don't want to be approached like that, yer know, because there must be other ways of doing it, because I'm going to say *no* to everything!"

Wasted words because the Beatles never again went into a recording studio together.

The struggle over space on the albums had a lot to do with growing musical differences amongst the Beatles. John and Paul had long since stopped collaborating, except for an occasional middle eight, even though all their compositions were still being published as "Lennon and McCartney." And George Harrison's songwriting had improved; his music had begun to be as popular as John's or Paul's, and it was understandable that he wanted equal time on the albums.

When the Beatles got together in the studio to record the double "White Album" and "Abbey Road," instead of closely collaborating with each other, as they had done in the old days, John, Paul and George each had their own separate songs to record. The session would turn into John with a backing group, Paul with a backing group, or George with a backing group. It became very clear whose songs were whose, which did not necessarily affect the overall feeling of the albums, but it created an uncertainty, a missing element; something was lacking—the spirit was broken within the group.

John's music had developed in a totally different direction than Paul's, toward the avant-garde and experimental. Paul, on the other hand, was immersed in his nostalgia-oriented "sweet" pop music. I knew that John was downright embarrassed by some of Paul's songs on the last few Beatles albums and hated being involved with them. He particularly disliked "Maxwell's Silver Hammer" on "Abbey Road" and "Ob-La-Di, Ob-La-Da" on the "White Album." When he told Paul this, Paul admitted that he was "not struck on them" either but that he had liked the songs when they were originally recorded.

John, Paul and George discussed this problem at Apple in the autumn of 1969, on one of the rare occasions when they got together. John glared at Paul and said, sarcastically: "It seemed mad for us to put a song on an album that nobody really dug, including the guy who wrote it, just because it was going to be popular, 'cause the LP doesn't have to be that. Wouldn't it be better, because we didn't really dig them, yer know, for you to do the songs you dug, and 'Ob-La-Di, Ob-La-Da' and 'Maxwell' to be given to people who like music like that, yer know, like Mary [Hopkins], or whoever it is needs a song. Why don't you give them to them? The only time we need anything vaguely near that quality is for a single. For an album we could just do only stuff that we really dug."

George's increasing success as a songwriter made John feel guilty that he and Paul hadn't given George more of a chance earlier, especially on the Beatles' singles, a lucrative market for the writer.

"We always carved the singles up between us," he told Paul. "We have the singles market, they [George and Ringo] don't get anything! I mean we've never offered George 'B' sides; we could have given him a lot of 'B' sides, but because we were two people you had the 'A' side and I had the 'B' side."

"Well the thing is," Paul answered, without even looking at George who sat a few feet away, "I think that until now, until this year [1969], our songs have been better than George's. Now this year his songs are at least as good as ours."

George was quick to correct Paul: "Now that's a myth, 'cause most of the songs this year I wrote about last year or the year before, anyway. Maybe now I just don't care whether you are going to like them or not, I just do 'em . . . If I didn't get a break I wouldn't push it, I'd just forget about it. Now for the last two years, at any rate, I've pushed it a bit more."

"I know what he's saying," John said, "'cause people have said to me you're coming through a lot stronger now than you had."

"I don't particularly seek acclaim," George said. "That's not the thing. It's just to get out whatever is there to make way for whatever else is there. You know, 'cause it's only to get 'em out, and also I might as well make a bit of money, seeing as I'm spending as much as the rest of you, and I don't earn as much as the rest of you!"

Like the others, George was now out on his own musically. "Most of my tunes," he said, "I never had the Beatles backing me."

"Oh! C'mon, George!" John shouted. "We put a lot of work in your songs, even down to "Don't Bother Me"; we spent a lot of time doing all that and we grooved. I can remember the riff you were playing, and in the last two years there was a period where you went Indian and we weren't needed!"

"That was only one tune," George said. "On the last album ["White Album"] I don't think you appeared on any of my songs—I don't mind."

John improvising, with George in the background, during the "Let It Be" sessions.

"Well, you had Eric [Clapton], or somebody like that," John replied, in a hurt tone of voice.

There was a long pause as each Beatle seemed lost in contemplation, wondering. Not wanting to admit that they were becoming individual musicians, Paul grasped at the remnants of truth and spoke slowly, almost whispering. "When we get in a studio, even on the worst day, I'm still playing bass, Ringo's still drumming, and we're still there you know."

But the drive, the determination, the combined energy and love of the group had gone. Instead of complimenting each other they now antagonized each other, and of course the music suffered. Yes, they were still there but only barely.

John's mood at this time is clearly reflected in the music he was writing, the long and ominous "I Want You, She's So Heavy" on the "Abbey Road" album and the painful "Cold Turkey," a song about heroin withdrawal. "Cold Turkey" really goes beyond just dealing with the pain of drug withdrawal to show John's despair over his realization that the Beatles were finished and that he was on his own. It also reveals his hurt and resentment of the abuse Yoko was receiving from everybody, his own blocked creativity and musical frustration: "Temperature's rising/Fever is high/Can't see no future/Can't see no sky/My feet are so heavy/So is my head/I wish I was a baby/I wish I was dead."

John had begun to realize that in order to record songs like "Cold Turkey" the way he wanted to, he had to use musicians who were completely behind *his* trip. The Toronto Rock 'n' Roll Revival served to reinforce his idea and pointed the way for the future.

Midafternoon on September 12, 1969, a call from Toronto came through to John's office at Apple, in the midst of a hectic schedule of press interviews. At first it seemed like one of the hundreds of harebrained schemes that were offered to John and Yoko every week. I accepted the call and listened to John Brower's proposal that John and Yoko attend the "biggest ever" Toronto Rock 'n' Roll Revival concert the next day to listen to such greats as Little Richard, Chuck Berry and Jerry Lee Lewis. He offered round-trip first class tickets for the couple and six of their friends. John, who was sitting across the desk from me, showed interest in the notes I was taking and stopped in midinterview to speak to the caller himself. He had hardly said hello before he was agreeing to go—on the condition that he and his band (which did not exist at that moment) could play *live* at the Revival. Brower was stunned;

he had never thought to ask such a thing—after all, none of the Beatles had played live in front of an audience since their last concert in San Francisco, in August 1966. He hastily assured John that the necessary immigration and visa documents would be taken care of. John seemed sceptical about this from past experience, but apparently Brower had the proper government connections.

Everything was set in motion pending Brower's call later that day to confirm the immigration details. John postponed the remaining interviews and set about organizing a band, the Plastic Ono Band, which could adequately back him the following evening on a stage three thousand miles away. He shouted to me: "Get me Eric [Clapton] on the phone, and then try to find Klaus [Voormann], he can play bass. And tell Mal that he's coming to organize the gear!" For a drummer, John decided on Alan White, a young session drummer who had been playing at Apple recently.

This really was a last-minute affair, as everybody had to be at the airport by ten the following morning for the flight to Toronto. The first problem was that Eric Clapton couldn't be located, although his agency swore that he was resting in his country cottage in the Berkshire Downs. I sent him a telegram in the hope that he would call John later that night.

The next question was what this hastily assembled band would perform. John didn't give the matter too much thought except to make a short list of the songs he wanted to sing, reasoning that they could rehearse during the six-hour flight. His main worry was remembering the words, even to his own songs, so he asked me to write them out in capitals on large sheets of Bag Production stationery. The songs included the newly written "Cold Turkey," oldies "Money" and "Blue Suede Shoes," and "Give Peace A Chance."

That this unlikely event might actually happen started to dawn on me when eight airline tickets were delivered to Apple and Brower called back from Toronto to confirm that the entry visas had been granted. The following morning, after a chaotic rush to round up the necessary equipment, everyone except for Eric and the Lennons was assembled at London Airport. There was one hour to go before take-off so I put a call through to Tittenhurst Park to see if John and Yoko were ready. Val, the cook, answered, and blurted out the news that they were still asleep and didn't want to be disturbed. I realized that despite all the arrangements our chances of seeing John Lennon on stage again were pretty remote. After much pleading on my part, Val finally agreed to go upstairs and bang on their door. Moments later John got on the line and confirmed my fear that they had copped out: "We couldn't wake up in time, and anyway Yoko doesn't feel well," he said. "Send them a telegram to cancel it—and send them a big bunch of white flowers, saying 'love and peace, John and Yoko.' "

Knowing their moods I took a chance, decided not to send either the telegram or the flowers, and asked everyone to stand by at the airport. I rushed over to Tittenhurst, hoping that with a little encouragement they would change their minds and go through with the concert. When I arrived they seemed more relaxed and in much better spirits, having just finished breakfast. John appeared to be getting his confidence back about performing, and at my suggestion that we could still catch a later flight there was a glimmer of enthusiasm. The clincher came when, with uncanny timing, Eric Clapton called to tell John that he could make it and was really keen to play.

Without a second thought about his earlier cancellation, everything was on again and John leapt out of bed, adrenalin rising, to choose his "stage suit"! Relieved and excited, I called the airport to break the good news to the waiting entourage and to set the wheels in motion for the Plastic Ono Band's Air Canada Flight No. 124 to Toronto. Everything from then on went smoothly; three hours later John and Yoko were in the air with Eric and the rest of the band.

On board John made a half-hearted attempt to rehearse a couple of songs with Eric and Klaus, showing them chords on an old acoustic guitar, but his mind was on heavier things, particularly his decision to leave the Beatles. During the flight he confided this to Eric and Klaus, even discussing ideas about them joining his "new" group.

Meanwhile, a few hours ahead of them across the Atlantic the airwaves over Canada were crackling with the news of John's imminent arrival to play LIVE. The freeways into Toronto were already jammed with kids from all over the country trying to attend this historic event, and traffic was backed up in the Detroit-to-Windsor auto tunnel as people began to arrive from the States.

By the time the plane touched down several hundred fans had gathered to welcome the band, and after clearing Immigration everybody ran down the exit tunnel in mock-Beatle fashion to the waiting black limousine. The Varsity Stadium was chaos. As we pulled in through the performers' entrance kids surged forward over the car, hammering on the windows and jumping up onto the hood. Security police finally cleared the way and we were escorted into a barricaded locker room, which was to serve as the stars' dressing room. The atmosphere was electric and everything felt weird and cold. It was nearly dark outside and the crowd was roaring with approval at Kim Fowley's announcement that John and Yoko and the Plastic Ono Band had arrived safely.

Sensing that the surrounding group of reporters, musicians and assorted hangers-on were about to descend on us, John demanded a private room and a small portable amp so that they could rehearse. The room was miniscule, damp, almost squalid. John was already showing his first signs of nervousness and paranoia at the prospect of being onstage again. While Eric plugged in his guitar and slumped into a corner John retreated into the restroom, where he threw up violently. The pain in his gut, he said, was unbearable.

But once onstage he plunged right into "Blue Suede Shoes," and when the crowd roared its support the Lennon magic started to flow. John was nervous but not noticeably so. His long hair flowing onto the shoulders of his white suit, he moved around the stage inspiring the group to a powerhouse level through "Money," and "Dizzy Miss Lizzy." The mood intensified as he sang his way through "Yer Blues" and a painful "Cold Turkey." Then the band launched into "Give Peace A Chance." Unable to remember half the words, John mumbled and ad-libbed, but it didn't matter—thousands of people were on their feet, chanting and swaying, singing with him. As a final appreciation the whole audience lit matches and held them above their heads, and the vast arena glowed. It was an exhilarating moment of instant rapport between John and his audience.

After the concert we were quickly driven away in a convoy of limousines to the country estate of Thor Eaton, a friend of one of the organizers, and spent the rest of the weekend relaxing amidst lakes and mountains.

Even after returning to London John remained excited about the Festival. He explained both his and Yoko's performance to rock writer Ritchie Yorke in *Rolling Stone*: "We did all the old things from the Cavern days in Liverpool. Gene Vincent was standing on the stage crying when we did our number. Backstage he came up to me and whispered: 'John, remember Hamburg? Remember all that scene?'

"The ridiculous thing was that I didn't know any of the lyrics. When we did 'Money' and 'Dizzy,' I just made up the words as I went along. The band was bashing it out like hell behind me. Yoko came up on stage with us, but she wasn't going to do her bit until we'd done our five songs. Then after 'Money' there was a stop, and I turned to Eric and said, 'what's next?' He just shrugged, so I screamed 'C'mon!' and started into something else. We did 'Yer Blues' because I've done that with Eric before. It blew our minds. Meanwhile Yoko had whipped off-stage to get some lyrics out of her white bag. Then we went into 'Give Peace A Chance,' which was just unbelievable. I was making up the words as we went along, I didn't have a clue. After that, we just wandered off to the back of the stage and we lit up and let go.

"Yoko's first number had a bit of rhythm but the second was completely freaky. It was the sort of thing she did at Cambridge '69 but it was more like Toronto 1984. . . . Yoko just stopped when she'd had enough, walked off, and we left all the amps on, going like clappers. Wow-ow-ow-ow! It went on for another five minutes, just flat. Then Mal Evans went out and turned them off."

The success of the Toronto performance gave John the confidence to play with other musicians who backed not only his music but also his ideas and energy. This pushed him even further away from the Beatles and in particular Paul. John was determined now to tell Paul and everyone else that this was it, the Beatles were over. He couldn't keep it inside any longer.

But it was not an easy decision. John went into a state of depression—deep down he was sick about the idea of leaving the group, but he really had no choice. He knew it would hurt, amputating, as he would have to, a part of himself. I watched him agonize for days over it—irritable, chain-smoking, and impossible to be around, skulking in his bedroom, losing himself in sleep or drugging himself with television.

Allen Klein, who at that time was probably closer to John than anyone else aside from Yoko, was horrified at the idea of John breaking up the Beatles, and persuaded him that the time was wrong to make a public announcement. It would be disastrous, Klein said, for the fragile web of business transactions underway to untangle the Beatles' finances and would in turn jeopardize John's own future away from the group. John, under the weight of Klein's persuasive tactics, gave in and agreed not to tell anybody, even Paul.

The pressure, however, was too great and at the beginning of October 1969, John had a confrontation with Paul, upstairs at Apple, during a business meeting. I was not present myself, since I was working in John's office two floors below. But it immediately became clear that momentous events had occurred when John burst into the room, red in the face and fuming with rage. "That's it—it's all over!" he shouted as he sank into the leather chair. It wasn't easy for me to get all the details from John immediately. Apparently, things had come to a head when Paul had been

February 1970: A freshly cropped John and Yoko pose with their wrecked Austin Maxi which they had had placed on a concrete pedestal in the grounds of Tittenhurst Park—the car had skidded off a narrow country road and crashed into a ditch while John had been driving, in Tongue, Sutherland, six months earlier.

too insistent about wanting the Beatles to do a television show and to go out on the road again. John had flatly refused, but Paul kept on and on, finally goading him until John exploded. In desperation he told Paul it was all over. He was leaving and wanted a "divorce" from the group. Paul couldn't believe what he heard and was badly shaken up. He was relieved, though, when John promised to keep his word to Klein and not make the decision public or turn it into a scandal. It was a crucial moment, but the inner fireworks were just beginning.

The bizarre course of the following few months reflected John's trauma over ending the Beatles. In January 1970, isolated in the wastelands of Denmark in the Cox farmhouse, it seemed as if everything finally shattered. In one devastating moment, after a week of strange events which appeared outside his control, John had his long flowing Beatle hair shaved off, leaving a close-cropped crewcut. When I saw him the next day I was stunned—it seemed as if his whole personality had changed. He had not only cut his hair but he had also cut his ties with the past, even to the extent of castrating his own peace campaign. That day, driving back through the snow-covered fields outside Aalborg, I knew that a phase of John's life had come to an end.

But it wasn't cut and dried. Nothing was ever cut and dried with John. In a peculiar way I felt he wanted to bleed, to feel the pain as long as he could. Since he had articulated his decision to leave the Beatles, and had thrown around ideas about forming a new group on that dramatic plane trip to Toronto, he had let it ride—except for the one explosive meeting with Paul. He hadn't brought it up again or pushed the issue. Perhaps he was hedging for time, reconsidering, wondering if the Beatle thing could still work—knowing in his heart that it couldn't, that it had run its course.

Six months passed after the crucial meeting with Paul. And then out of the blue, in April 1970, after not speaking to John for months, Paul called him and said: "I'm doing what you and Yoko are doing, I'm putting out an album and I'm leaving the group *too!*" That was it, short and precise, typically Paul McCartney. In one breath, one sentence, he did what John had been trying to do for a whole year. Finish the Beatles once and for all. End the myth. John took it calmly at first: "I said good, you know, I was feeling a little strange because *he* was saying it this time, and I said good because he was the one that wanted the Beatles most." But next morning when John saw the headlines in all the daily papers that Paul had quit the Beatles to put out his own record, he felt a twinge of bitterness. Here was Paul making an "event" out of leaving the group, doing exactly what he had pleaded with John not to do just six months before.

John was confused, even though he had wanted the break-up so badly, now that it had happened the emotional intensity of the Beatles' end hit him hard. He withdrew again into the cold, reclusive state that I had come to accept as one of his character traits, having witnessed it so many times before—when he and Yoko had suffered abuse from both friends and the press; the miscarriages; the drug bust; the burden of the peace effort—the list seemed endless. John's personal crisis thus reached a breaking point, and it was not to be resolved until after Primal Therapy.

THE DREAM IS OVER

John Lennon's sensitivity to other people invariably left him vulnerable to their aggression. Early in 1970, in addition to his despair that the Beatles really were finished, there were mounting tensions in his relationship with Yoko, which became more destructive day by day. He retreated into passivity and inertia. Like one of Nin's characters, John had reached the point where his life "hung like a frayed cloth and the street of dreams turned into darkness."

This was an unhappy time at Tittenhurst Park. John and Yoko took the only escape they knew from pain and anxiety and hid in each other's love. But rapidly it became an obsessive, possessive love; without realizing it they were stifling each other.

"We'd be together twenty-four hours a day," John admitted. "That was our love, to protect our love—we were really beginning to choke each other. . . . We were in danger of being, I don't know, Zelda and Scott [Fitzgerald]. . . . We were happy and we were close, but we would have just—we're both balmy people. We would have blown up in a few years, couldn't have kept up the pace we were going at."

Living with them became harder day by day. Besides Val the cook I was the only person around and I was acutely aware of the rapid deterioration of their relationship. When they were depressed both John and Yoko would overreact to any little problem. Often I found myself in the middle of heated emotional outbursts, which left me sad and disoriented.

While John and Yoko remained secluded in their bedroom, the rest of the house resounded with frantic activity. Builders were hard at work making renovations, but sometimes would have to halt for days, waiting for John and Yoko to approve a certain alteration before work could continue. When the workmen got too noisy and it came time for the kitchen to be rebuilt John and Yoko moved out of Tittenhurst and stayed in a suite at a luxury hotel in Mayfair.

John escaped from his problems by watching television. It seemed as if he didn't really care where he was as long as there was a color television at the foot of the bed. He didn't have any favorite programs but preferred to switch channels constantly, as his concentration level was low. He often said he preferred the commercials to anything else. Occasionally he would take words or phrases or simply abstract ideas from television and incorporate them into his songs.

But even during his worst bouts with depression and through all their quarreling John's love for Yoko was constant, and often touching. Yoko's birthday came during one of their stays at the Inn on the Park Hotel and John planned a surprise for her. She woke up to a beautiful bouquet of red roses and then every hour, all day long, more roses were delivered to the suite. By evening you could hardly walk through the place and the aroma from the forest of roses was overpowering. Yoko was ecstatic.

Once back at Tittenhurst John and Yoko again isolated themselves, communicating with no one. In part, I saw their withdrawal as a reaction to the frantic pace of the year before, the continual dialogue with the media, the peace efforts, all the traveling. Also, although he didn't realize it at the time, John desperately needed somebody else to turn to, someone to help him besides Yoko, who acted as his only outlet. It was obvious to me that their relationship could not continue much longer the way it was going.

But a book arrived in the mail one morning which precipitated a chain of events that changed John and Yoko's lives radically. The book was *The Primal Scream (Primal Therapy: The Cure for Neurosis)* by Arthur Janov, an American psychologist, and it presented a new approach to psychological thinking.

"This man's book came in the post," said John, "and when I read it I thought it was like Newton's apple. 'This must be it!' I said. But I'd been so wrong in the past, with the drugs and with the Maharishi . . . that I gave it to Yoko. She agreed with me, so we got on the phone. . . ."

In his book Janov claimed to have discovered *the* cure for neurosis. *The Primal Scream* describes his method for transforming neurotics into "real" human beings. Neurosis to Janov means defenses; Primal Therapy is designed to strip patients of all defenses.

Janov contends that the defenses (neuroses) are born out of the child's unfulfilled needs, especially his need for love. The child struggles desperately and in vain to please his parents and be loved by them. Finally his unfulfilled needs are blocked from consciousness as a matter of self-preservation, so that the child stops feeling the pain they cause. But the price is tension and neurosis, and the replacement of real needs by symbolic needs. As long as the pain of unfulfilled needs is repressed, behavior will be unreal and neurotic. Only experiencing and working through Primal pain permits the person to get back into contact with his real needs and become a real person again.

After several phone conversations with John and Yoko, Janov agreed to fly to London and begin the therapy. Everything came to a standstill; any projects underway were stopped. Janov's instructions to John and Yoko to prepare themselves for Primal Therapy were difficult, but essential. They were asked to separate from each other twenty-four hours before the first session and to be completely alone in a room with no television, radio or phone. They were just allowed to have pencil and paper to write with. Yoko stayed in the bedroom and John went to the other end of the house and took over the half completed studio. It was the first time they had been apart from each other for over two years.

When Janov arrived I was surprised by his warmth and youthful appearance. He had the presence and aura of a Hollywood movie star rather than that of a psychiatrist, but I instinctively felt that John and Yoko would get on well with him. The initial stage of Primal Therapy took three weeks; Janov had a session with John and Yoko separately, every day. After the first week at Tittenhurst Park it was decided that everyone should move up to London. John took a suite at the Inn on the Park Hotel. I went with Yoko, who was in a fragile and nervous state, and checked her into the Londonderry, a few yards down the street.

"The first few days of therapy," writes Janov, "seem to parallel the first few years of the patient's life, before the occurrence of the Primal Scene that shut him down. He experiences isolated and discreet events in bits and pieces. As each fragment combines into a meaningful whole, the patient goes into his primal."

In John's case the layers of hurt had been building up since he was five, when he was forced to make a choice between his father and mother. He chose his father, then at the last minute ran after his mother, only to be taken to his Aunt Mimi's house to be brought up. When a teenager John got to know his mother again, but just as she was becoming his closest friend she was killed by a car in the street right outside his house.

The pain of his mother's death was so deep and so traumatic that John never let himself really feel it until therapy. His body shut down to the intolerable pain, requiring something to keep it hidden and suppressed. Neurosis served this function; it diverted John from his pain, and the

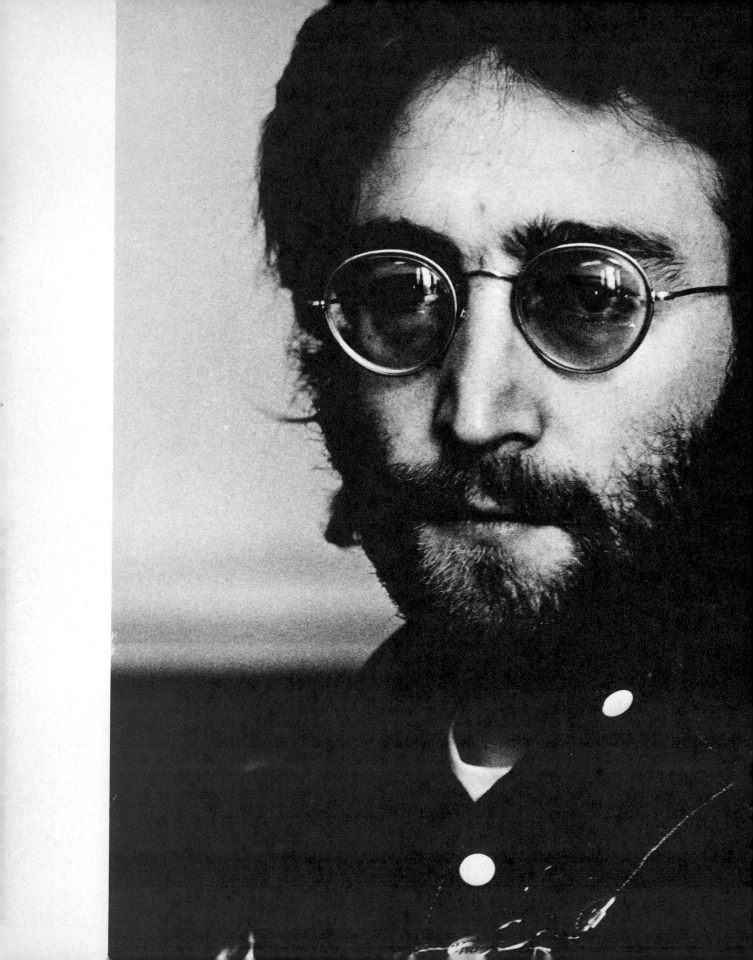

John as "Working Class Hero," photographed after primal therapy at the time of his thirty-thousand-word interview for *Rolling Stone*.

resulting urgent yet unfulfilled needs were channeled into his music.

The layers of tension stored inside John finally *were* released as he slowly made the connection with their origins. For twenty-nine years he had buried the hurt, the fear, the aloneness. Now he could feel the pain and his own feelings, and he started writing songs again. They are evidence of what he was going through. In "Mother" he wrote: "Mother, you had me but I never had you,/I wanted you, but you didn't want me. . . ./Father, you left me but I never left you,/I needed you but you didn't need me." And in "Isolation": "Just a boy and a little girl,/Trying to change the whole wide world/Isolation. . . ./We're afraid of everyone/Afraid of the sun/Isolation."

At the end of the three weeks Janov explained to John and Yoko that they would have to go to the Primal Institute in California if they wanted to complete the therapy, because the whole process took four to six months to be really effective. An important part of Primal Therapy was joining in group sessions. There Post-Primal groups met twice weekly and their function was to stimulate group members into new Primals.

Both John and Yoko understood that this was just the beginning and since they were amazed at what was happening to them, they readily agreed to go to California and continue the therapy.

The Ascot mansion, Tittenhurst Park, was locked up, the office at Apple closed down and John and Yoko left for the Primal Institute in Los Angeles. They stayed for four months and when not attending group sessions would hide out in their Bel Air rented house, soothed by the continual flicker of the TV set at the foot of the bed, or escape for raids on the local ice cream parlors. Janov had said: "Don't control yourself in any way—do what your body wants." The therapy was difficult but re-warding as all their defenses were slowly broken down and the ghosts of unloving parents exorcised.

"The thing in a nutshell," said John, "[is that] Primal Therapy allowed us to feel feelings continually, and those feelings usually make you cry. That's all. Because before I wasn't feeling things. I was blocking the feelings."*

John, however, did not emerge "cured." Although the pain was not taken away, he underwent a significant growth experience that was both rewarding and important: he developed the ability to isolate and feel his own pain. Post-Primal John Lennon was in more pain when he left California than before, but now he could channel it and work with it. The

*Lennon Remembers: The Rolling Stone Interviews, Straight Arrow Books, San Francisco, 1971.

immediate result was the writing and recording of a group of unashamedly honest and raw songs which were to become an important musical statement. All the years of compressed feelings and denied needs and the violence of wrenching them out of an unreal system he translated intimately into his first solo album, "John Lennon/Plastic Ono Band," which he recorded in England immediately after coming out of therapy. Brilliantly fused into the songs are his innermost feelings—the bitterness, the hatred and realizations of the past, encapsuled in lyrics so powerful that I can only find parallels in art—in Van Gogh's tortured canvases where every painful brushstroke speaks from the gut, in Jackson Pollock's frenzied expressionist abstracts—so John painted his songs with each word, each note pulled from his inner anguish.

John expressed his pain at being a "Working Class Hero": "When they've tortured and scared you for twenty odd years/Then they expect you to pick a career/When you can't really function you're so full of fear . . ." Coproduced by Phil Spector, but without the least trace of his full sound, the record is very tight musically, relying mainly on the delicate balance between John's aggressive vocals and his primitive choked guitar playing.

Essentially the album is about pain and reality. The old imagery is gone, as are the fantasies and acid revelations. It is John as naked mentally as he had been physically on the "Two Virgins" cover.

John felt that this album, released in October 1970, was a peak for him, a kind of "Sergeant Lennon." He said at the time in *Lennon Remembers*: "I don't really know how it will sink in, where it will lie in the spectrum of rock 'n' roll and the generation and the rest of it. . . . I don't know whether it's going to settle down in a minority position . . . it could do that because in one way it's terribly uncommercial, it's so miserable in a way and so heavy, but it's reality and I'm not going to veer away from it for anything."*

John and Yoko were happy again. They felt that the therapy had helped them to build up more of a friendship and understanding; they felt fresh, invigorated, almost reborn. John had shattered all the illusions. In "God," he listed all the things he didn't believe in, ending with: "I don't believe in Beatles/I just believe in me/Yoko and me/And that's reality."

John's strength and endurance were evident in the effort he made to work through his inner traumas and to reach another level of awareness. His message could not have been clearer: ". . . I was the walrus/But now I'm John/And so dear friends/You just have to carry on/The dream is over."

John and Yoko lie against a medieval tree in the grounds of Tittenhurst Park at the time of recording the "John Lennon/Plastic Ono Band" album.

*Lennon Remembers: The Rolling Stone Interviews. Straight Arrow Books, San Francisco, 1971.

MEAT CITY-NEW YORK

"I like to live in the land of the free, and also if it's up to Joe Doe on the street, he either doesn't care about it or would be glad to have an old Beatle living here. I like to be here cos this is where the music came from, this is what influenced my whole life and got me where I am today as it were. And I love the place and I'd like to be here—I've got a lot of friends here, and this is where I want to be! Statue of Liberty welcome—I even brought my own cash!"   (John Lennon, 1975)

America was a legend to John long before he ever left England's shores. In his imagination it held pride of place as the mythical land that had spawned rock 'n' roll and was the home of his idol, Elvis Presley. "In Liverpool," he loved to say, "when you stood on the edge of the water you knew the next place was America." But the culture itself was no myth: like many other English kids John was brought up on Kellogg's Cornflakes, Heinz Baked Beans, Coca-Cola and Hollywood movies. When the Beatles' dream came true and they toured all over the States John was overwhelmed, although it was impossible for him to feel the true pulse of the cities while shut away in hotel rooms or stuck in the back of black-windowed limousines.

The reasons for the Lennons 1971 move to New York were numerous and complex, a series of events rather than any specific decision on the part of John or Yoko. Initially they came to the United States in an effort to locate Yoko's daughter, Kyoko, who had once again disappeared with her father Tony Cox. For several years, losing and then relocating Kyoko had been a frustrating exercise for the Lennons. They were now determined to do something about it once and for all by taking the case to the American courts so that Yoko could appeal for custody of the child.

Cox was in the habit of getting in touch with John and Yoko every time he needed money; however he was concerned about Yoko staying with them for extended periods; he felt very strongly that their environment and lifestyle would not be good for her. On the surface Yoko appeared content to have only occasional meetings, but deep down I think she felt the pain of separation and each time she lost contact with her daughter

"America is where it's at. I should have been born
in New York….Everybody heads towards the center,
that's why I'm here now. I'm just here to breathe
it…it's so overpowering, America," said John.

she would lapse into periods of intense anxiety. After a while finding Kyoko became an obsession, the main priority in Yoko's life. This quest had earlier led John and Yoko to Denmark and now it led them to the Virgin Islands and New York.

New York had been Yoko's home for fifteen years before she met John, and from her descriptions and many stories John had gradually built up a strong desire to experience the city firsthand. In England Yoko lived very much in John's domain, and I felt that she was itching to get back to the big city among the artistic avant-garde. In 1969 they had been denied entry into the States because of John's drug conviction and I had shuttled back and forth to New York on their behalf. Finally they were allowed to stay in the country during the spring and summer of 1970 to undergo Primal Therapy.

Toward the end of the same year, after returning to England to record the "John Lennon/Plastic Ono Band" album, John and Yoko visited New York together for the first time. It was an enlightening experience for John—he got to meet many artists and filmmakers including Jonas Mekas, and he spent a lot of time with Allen Klein.

John was interviewed during this visit by Jann Wenner, editor of *Rolling Stone.* The result was an impressive thirty thousand word article which was run in two parts, under the title of "John Lennon, The Working Class Hero." The interview presented the public with a rare detailed insight into John's inner feelings of that moment. It was read in context with his new record and both reflected the thoughts and realizations Post-Primal Lenon had arrived at after four months of intense therapy.

John was definitely hooked on New York. Ten years earlier he had loved night life in Hamburg, the all-night cafes and nightclubs, the fun of getting anything you wanted day or night. Liverpool also was a cosmopolitan bustling port full of immigrants and nightclubs where blues and rock 'n' roll were played. So in spirit John was really a New Yorker long before he arrived. He told Wenner at the end of his visit: "America is where it's at. I should have been born in New York, I should have been born in the Village, that's where I belong. . . . Everybody heads toward the centre, that's why I'm here now. I'm here just to breathe it . . . it's so overpowering, America, and I'm such a fuckin' cripple that I can't take much of it, it's too much for me."*

John and Yoko returned to England. Eight months later, after recording the "Imagine" album in the recently completed studios at Tittenhurst Park and shooting forty thousand feet of film to go with it, the Lennons went to the Virgin Islands, where Kyoko and Tony Cox were reported to

*Lennon Remembers: The Rolling Stone Interviews, Straight Arrow Books, San Francisco, 1971.

be living, and then on to New York. This time they were not to leave and the city was to become their home for many years.

They rented a studio in the West Village to live in and a loft in Soho to use as a workspace. John felt comfortable in the Village: "It's like a little Welsh village, with Jones the Fish and Jones the Milk, and everybody seems to know everybody." And he quickly got into New York habits like riding a bicycle in the Park, going to movies in the middle of the night, and picking up the Sunday papers in Sheridan Square. "We love it," John said. "New York *is* a fantastic place; there's an unbelievably creative atmosphere on this little island of Manhattan. Like they say, there just isn't anything you can't get in New York. . . . I love all the gear here, whether it's cheeseburgers or more TV channels. There's definitely more energy in America, and I don't think it's the size of the country or the amount of people here. It's just that Americans have more energy. America is more my speed."

POWER TO THE PEOPLE

"I got off the boat, only it was an aeroplane, and landed in New York, and the first people who got in touch with me was Jerry Rubin and Abbie Hoffman. It's as simple as that. It's those two famous guys from America who's callin: 'Hey, yeah, what's happenin', what's goin' on? . . .' And the next thing you know I'm doin' John Sinclair benefits and one thing and another. I'm pretty *movable*, as an artist, you know. They almost greeted me off the plane and the next minute I'm *involved*."   (John Lennon, 1975)

After "Instant Karma," John's tongue-in-cheek idea of "instant" enlightenment, it just might be possible to imagine him seduced into becoming an instant radical. He did become immediately involved with Rubin and Hoffman and the radical New Left, but it wasn't quite as simple as that. John is receptive to other peoples' ideas and has often been coerced into causes that are in no way *his* causes, but for this to happen there has to be a common wavelength, and the germ of an idea already forming in the back of his mind.

John's transformation from an advocate of love and peace to an angry politico had actually begun six months before he arrived in New York and became embroiled in the highly charged atmosphere of the "Movement." He was in a dilemma over actual violence: "What can you do? What can you do?" he kept asking. "You can't take power without a struggle. Because when it comes to the nitty gritty they won't let the people have any power, they'll give all the rights to perform and to dance for them, but no real power. I don't know what the answer is."

On his "John Lennon/Plastic Ono Band" album John had expressed his

John and Yoko walk around the West Village feeling very much at home. Bottom left: Their first studio apartment on Bank Street in the Village.

anger over the fact that nothing had really changed, that in spite of all the peace demonstrations and youth protests the same people still controlled the system. He began to realize that the only way to effect a peaceful revolution was to start with the kids and the young workers: "That's why I talk about school on the album. I'd like to incite people to break the framework, to be disobedient in school, to stick their tongues out, to insult authority."

John had been concerned about the idea of revolution for a long time but he had always approached the subject with hesitation. When he recorded "Revolution" in 1968, he made two versions. One said "Count me *in*," the other said "count me *out*." "I put in both because I wasn't sure . . ." he said. "I didn't want to get killed. I didn't really know that much about the Maoists, but I just knew that they seemed to be so few and yet they painted themselves green and stood in front of the police waiting to get picked off. . . . That was how I felt—I was really asking a question. As someone from the working class I was always interested in Russia and China and everything that related to the working class, even though I was playing the capitalist game."

In February 1971, John recorded "Power to the People," a hypnotic song with a simple, driving message. It was a slogan, it was youth graffiti, but it reflected the moment. "I began to realize that we are all oppressed, which is why I would like to do something about it, though I'm not sure where my place is," John told the leftwing magazine *Red Mole*. He felt strongly about the oppression of the workers, and came to the conclusion that the only solution was to make them aware of their really unhappy position: "They're dreaming someone else's dream, it's not even their own. They should realize that the blacks and the Irish are being harassed and repressed and that they will be next. As soon as they can start being aware of all that, we can really begin to do something. The workers can start to take over."

The English press construed John's comments as extreme leftwing and even communist. In reply he retaliated: "They knock me for saying 'Power to the People' and say that no one section should have the power. Rubbish. The people aren't a section. The people means everyone. I think that everyone should own everything equally and that the people should own part of the factories and they should have some say in who is the boss and who does what. Students should be able to select teachers. It might be like communism but I don't really know what real communism is. There is no real communist state in the world—you must realize that Russia isn't. It's a fascist state. The socialism I talk about is British socialism, not where some daft Russian might do it. That might

John becomes an angry politico. Top left: With Jerry Rubin the night of the Attica benefit at the Apollo Theater; bottom left: With Jerry Rubin at a press conference.

John and Yoko during a quiet moment while playing with Elephant's Memory.

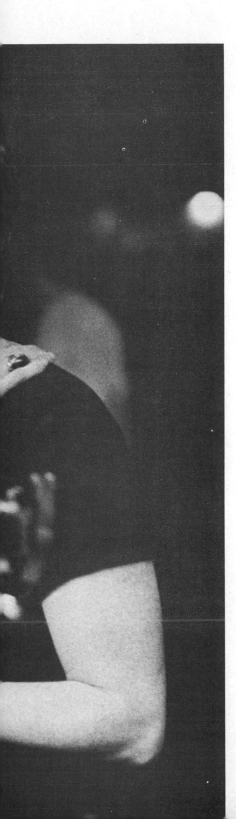

suit them. Us, we'd have a nice socialism here. A British socialism.''

The "Imagine" album, recorded immediately before John and Yoko moved to New York, revealed more of John's increasingly radical ideas. In "Gimme Some Truth," he sang about "neurotic psychotic pigheaded politicians" and warned that "no short haired yellow bellied son of tricky dickey is gonna mother hubbard soft soap me with just a pocketful of hope . . ." And in the poignant "Imagine," John conceptualized his vision of the much discussed peaceful revolution: "Imagine there's no countries/it isn't hard to do/nothing to kill or die for/and no religion too/ imagine all the people/living life in peace/no need for greed or hunger/a brotherhood of man/Imagine all the people/sharing all the world. . . ."

So it was really no coincidence that John tied up with "crazies like Jerry Rubin and Abbie-my-boy-Hoffman," as he called them. He was ripe for action, living in New York was a new experience, and he wanted desperately to be accepted, to be involved in what was happening. Since therapy John had been pretty much of a recluse, getting fat and living in his two identical pairs of workman's overalls. New York was an instant release, it energized him. He wanted to play music so badly that any excuse served the purpose; the Attica relatives' benefit found him standing up in the Apollo with his guitar and he was happy to jump onstage at the John Sinclair rally at Ann Arbor.

John started hanging out with a group called Elephant's Memory and with their help he and Yoko put together "Sometime in New York City," a double album musical diary of their radical involvement. They sang about Angela Davis, John Sinclair, the Attica prison revolt, the war in Northern Ireland and women's liberation. As a propaganda album it worked, and was a natural progression in John's career. It was also the first record that John and Yoko successfully worked on together. Five of the songs were vocal collaborations, three written by Yoko and two by John. The music was strong and vibrant, much of the album had the spontaneity and impact of a live performance. The critics' unanimous dislike of the album was harsh, and for the most part, I felt, unwarranted. "Woman is the Nigger of the World" was certainly a brave and important song.

Looking back at the negative response, John said: "That's when I got into the so-called 'political songs,' which I don't think are the best songs I've ever written, because I was trying too hard—but the *concept* I was trying to get over was writing about what the people are saying now. And that's what I lost myself in—by not writing what *I* was thinking and saying. It worked in 'Give Peace A Chance,' but it didn't work in other songs.'' Considering his musical progression John felt strongly that this period of radicalism was detrimental to his work: "It almost *ruined* it, in a way. It became journalism and not poetry. And I basically *feel* that I'm a poet. . . . And I realized that over a period of time—and not just 'cause I met Jerry Rubin off the plane—but that was like a culmination. I realized that *we were poets but we were really folk poets*, and rock and roll was folk poetry—I've always felt that. . . . Then I began to take it seriously on another level, saying, 'Well, I am reflecting what is going *on*, right?' And then I was making an *effort* to reflect what was going on. . . . It doesn't work as pop music or what I want to do. It just doesn't make sense."

JOHN LENNON VS. THE U.S.

A secret, hysterical White House report lay behind John's dispute with the U.S. Immigration authorities. Former President Nixon personally ordered Government officials to harass him and "kick him out of America." John had no idea what he was getting himself into when he became involved almost overnight with Rubin and Hoffman. Within a few months after he began appearing publicly at radical events and benefits his phones were tapped, his rooms bugged, and he was followed everywhere he went. The thought of a Beatle political activist was more than the Nixon "police state" could stand. They feared he was becoming a "guerilla in the field of culture."

In early 1972, the staff of the Senate Internal Security Subcommittee of the Judiciary Committee prepared and submitted to Senator Strom Thurmond a remarkable memorandum about John. The inflammatory six-paragraph memo, headed "John Lennon," noted that John had appeared at a 1971 rally for John Sinclair in Ann Arbor and then added that Rennie Davis, Jerry Rubin, Leslie Bacon, Stu Albert, Jay Craven and "others" had recently gone to New York City. "This group," said the memo, "has been strong advocates of the program to 'dump Nixon.' They have devised a plan to hold rock concerts in various primary election states for the following purposes: to obtain access to college campuses; to stimulate 18-year-old registration; to press for legislation legalizing marihuana; to finance their activities; and to recruit persons to come to San Diego during the Republican National Convention in August 1972. These individuals are the same persons who were instrumental in disrupting the Democratic National Convention in Chicago in 1968. . . . Davis and his cohorts intend to use John Lennon as a drawing card to promote the success of the rock festivals and rallies. The source feels that this will pour tremendous amounts of money into the coffers of the New Left and can only inevitably lead to a clash between a controlled mob organized by this group and law enforcement officials in San Diego. The source felt that if Lennon's visa is terminated it would be a strategy counter-measure."

On February 4, 1972, Senator Thurmond wrote to John Mitchell attaching the memo. "This appears to me to be an important matter, and I think it would be well for it to be considered at the highest level," he wrote. "As I can see many headaches might be avoided if appropriate action be taken in time." Handwritten at the bottom was this afterthought: "I also sent Bill Timmons [a White House aide] a copy of the memorandum."

Mitchell turned the affair over to deputy attorney general Kleindienst, who on February 14, 1972 wrote to Immigration and Naturalization Service (INS) commissioner Raymond Farrell: "Ray, please call me about the attached. When is he coming? Do we—if we so elect—have any basis to deny his admittance?" They did, and the INS moved to revoke John's visa because of the 1968 drug arrest in England. Farrell's associate commissioner, James Greene, called New York INS district director, Sol Marks, on March 2, 1972, and told him to "immediately revoke the voluntary departure granted to John Lennon and his wife." He further directed Marks to disapprove Lennon's preliminary application to remain in the country, adding that it was a personal request from Farrell. On March 6, 1972 the visa extension granted to John just five days earlier was duly revoked. "It is understood that you have no intention of effecting your departure," Marks wrote to John.

John himself knew nothing of these details at the time. He was aware only that the government was using the technicality of his drug arrest to get him out of the country. The case disrupted all his plans, but he was determined to fight to stay in the country. Yoko's custody of Kyoko was still to be resolved and John had been planning to go on the road with Elephant's Memory. On April 29, 1972, John Lindsay, then Mayor of New York, asked federal authorities to allow John and Yoko to remain permanently in America, and to quash the deportation proceedings. "A grave injustice is being perpetrated," he said.

For John there was pain and confusion: "In '72, it was really gettin' to me. Not only was I physically having to appear in court cases, it just seemed like a toothache that wouldn't go away. But there was just a period where I *just couldn't function,* you know? I was so paranoid from them tappin' the phone and followin' me. . . . How could I prove that they were tappin' me phone? There was no way. And when they were followin' me, I went on 'Dick Cavett' and said they were followin' me and they stopped. But when they *were* followin' me, they wanted me to *see* they were following me. I was so damn paranoid.''

Not only was there illegal interference from the White House in John's immigration case, there were also plans for a big political trial—to show through his songs, ideas, and even his friends, that John was unfit to be a resident of the United States. The idea was tossed around in the office of Sol Marks, but Vincent Schiano, a government lawyer assigned to the case, argued that such a trial would be a disaster—it would create ill feeling among young people, and was unnecessary legally. It was easy for the government to get rid of Lennon, Schiano declared. Either he had or did not have a criminal record, and if he had one he was out. Why bother with the songs? The crux of the matter was that Nixon and his top aides in Washington were afraid that John would disrupt the 1972 Republican National Convention in San Diego, and for that reason they had applied pressure on the local immigration people in New York.

In March 1973, John was again ordered to leave the U.S. by immigration authorities. He replied: ''Having just celebrated our fourth wedding anniversary, we are not prepared to sleep in separate beds. Peace and love, John and Yoko.'' Everything hinged on the drug arrest, which John always maintained had been a ''plant'' anyway. He tried asking the Queen for a Royal Pardon, ''so as to be free to travel to and from the United States,'' but his request was denied.

The following year the fight was stepped up. On July 18, 1974, the U.S. Justice Department ordered John to leave the country within sixty days or be deported, after the Immigration Service had denied an extension of his nonimmigrant visa. But then a news item changed everything, exploded the whole scene: Jack Anderson revealed in his column that the Immigration effort to get rid of John was not because of the pot bust but because of his outspoken opposition to the Vietnam War, and the false rumor that he was going to lead a demonstration against Nixon at the Republican Convention. The tip of the iceberg was now public; it was hoped that the details would follow. Immediately John's lawyers started proceedings against the government in Federal Court: ''My immigration lawyer is suing the government—I am, I suppose—for wiretapping, for not being nice, not playing it like cricket, you know,'' John explained. ''Then there is an appeal—that is, my appeal. . . . It seems to be like any law case only they're not fighting about the money. It's up there, something conceptual. The result is a concept, right? . . . When the lawyer calls me and tells me it's time to do something then I do it. Otherwise, I just forget all about it and don't deal with it. I'm keeping positive. I'm going to be here and ain't nothing going to get me out. So however they do it is up to them. Whatever ritual they want to go through, I'm not going anywhere."

The Board of Immigration Appeals ordered John to leave voluntarily by September 8, 1974, or be deported. He lodged another appeal. By this time the Immigration people had started to change their tactics, emphasizing the fact that John had "overstayed" his original visa period. "When they started the initial case," John said, "they claimed that it was a local New York problem, and they also started the proceedings against John and Yoko. Halfway through they discovered that actually Yoko did not have any record in England and actually she had a 'green card' by a previous American husband. So this 'local case' that was just like any other alien, which is what they kept claiming, was not one of those cases—so then they suddenly had to find something else, which was this 'overstay' business, with which they pulled a fast one. Now one of them (Greene) keeps writing to the papers saying they're still treating me like a normal citizen—alien—only on overstay, no longer mentioning about marijuana and the original normal reason I was being thrown out. It's just interesting that the case keeps changing to suit them."

John and Yoko at the "One to One" concert at Madison Square Garden, August 30, 1972.

Apart from his difficulties with Immigration, John followed through on his plans to live and work in the U.S. On August 30, 1972, he did two benefit concerts for retarded children at Madison Square Garden. After television rights were sold and the federal government's matching funds added, the receipts totaled $1.5 million. The money was given to three New York charities to build small residences where retarded children could receive individual attention. To emphasize this idea the concern was named "One to One," and mayor Lindsay declared August 30 "One to One" day.

The night of the concert John was in a very good mood and for the second show especially, he gave a memorable performance. It was clear that he could be as pungent, versatile, and powerful a performer as he had been in previous years; in fact, he surprised everyone with his sharpness and versatility. It was after midnight when John and Yoko came on, spotlighted in front of a horseshoe of amplifiers. They were backed by the powerful Elephant's Memory band, supplemented by Jim Keltner on drums and also a second bass player. John was dressed in a green army fatigue jacket, chewed gum constantly and swung his guitar around in obvious enjoyment and enthusiasm. They did sixteen songs in all, but John had the most fun with rockers like "Come Together" and "Instant Karma," (which he and Yoko performed at adjoining electric pianos); their strong version of "Cold Turkey" was totally electrifying. John ges-

The tumultuous ending of "Give Peace A Chance" at the "One to One" concert. All the musicians joined John and Elephant's Memory onstage, and afterwards the audience gave a five-minute standing ovation (above).

ticulated and rock 'n' rolled his way through the song, his lyrics really alive and their meaning suddenly crystal clear.

They also gave an impromptu performance of "Hound Dog," with John screaming and knocking his knees together. The concert came to a tumultuous end with a reggae version of "Give Peace A Chance," during which everyone crowded onto the stage to join in. John put on a red tin Japanese worker's helmet, and the song went on forever until the audience finally ended it by giving John a long standing ovation.

In November 1973, John recorded "Mind Games," an album that expressed his mood and concentrated once again on his own thoughts and emotions, a relief after the slogans of "Sometime in New York City." "Mind Games" was both persuasive and lyrical, the synthesis that was John Lennon rather than the work of an agitprop musician relaying messages. The music, too, was refreshing in that it was imaginative, lush, and cohesive. He made the record after he realized suddenly that a year had gone by since his previous one. Its imagery reflected a renewed optimism and positive approach toward life. On "Only People" and "Intuition," John was radiant with a reaffirmed happiness.

" 'Mind Games' to me," John said, "was like an interim record, between being a manic political lunatic and back to being a musician again." The political issues were still there although cloaked in John's personal imagery, and subsidiary to a new attitude: "Keep on playing those mind games forever."

The lyrics of "Intuition" are tight; no words are wasted, every line has meaning in the autobiographical context. In just a few words John summed up his thinking: "My intentions are good, I use my intuition. It takes me for a ride. . . . And I play the game of life—I try to make it better each and every day. . . . And time after time confirmed an old suspicion—It's good to be alive."

By the winter of 1973 the immigration problems had become a constant strain on John and Yoko's relationship. Very quietly John just walked out one day and didn't go back. "As a friend said, I went out for coffee and some papers and I didn't come back," John said. "It's not a matter of *who* broke it up. *It* broke up."

To escape from his pain and loneliness, John flew to Los Angeles and immediately looked up Phil Spector. He thought Spector would be the perfect producer for an "oldies" record album, an idea he had been thinking about since finishing "Mind Games." "I've had enough of this to

Harry Nilsson (left) shooting pool with John.

After being ejected from the Los Angeles Troubadour Club, Harry and John were in a fighting mood.

be deep and think,'' he had decided. ''Why can't I have some fun?'' His idea of having fun was basically to be allowed to *sing,* and if he had a choice, to sing rock 'n' roll: ''Whenever I sang in a studio, when I wasn't singing my own *deep personal thoughts,* it was to sing rock 'n' roll— which is what I started with. I thought—'I know what I'll do, I'll make a rock 'n' roll album of all the songs I'm always singing in the studio, in be- tween takes, and I don't even want to be the producer or the writer.' ''

It took John three weeks of talking to persuade Spector that he could do it, and that it wasn't going to be a coproduction like ''Imagine,'' where John never let go of the control. He told Spector: ''I just wanna be Ronnie Spector or the Chiffons or whoever it is and I'll just sit there and sing, and I'm not even gonna come in until you've got it on the tape and then I'll come in. I'm not going to check the bass drum or anything—it's gonna be like you want it and I'll just do singing!''

The sessions started off well but gradually became more brandy than music: ''It was great at first—there he was being like the Phil Spector that I never allowed him to be, in complete control of twenty-eight guys play- ing, live, and to me, and to a lot of us who hadn't been there originally, it was like seeing the Spector sessions of the early sixties, which none of us saw. And he was fantastic, but it got madder and madder and it ended up breaking down and just falling apart.''

Spector locked up the tapes in his house where John couldn't get them, and then John found out that Spector had also paid for the sessions through Warner Brothers. This didn't make any sense because all his ses- sions are automatically paid for by E.M.I. or Capitol. John said: ''So the next minute not only had the sessions collapsed but I haven't the tapes, and the having fun fell into having no fun—so then I was hanging around L.A. for months and months, waiting for him to come out of his hole, and there's all these stories about 'he's had an accident,' or 'he's dying,' and you never know what to believe cos he lives an incredible surreal life in his own head!''

John tried to rationalize this turn of events by thinking, ''I'm crazy, he's crazy—and he's crazier than me, that's all.'' But then he began to be fed up, especially with all the drinking, and got very depressed about having no tapes. Also, being separated from Yoko for the first time since the beginning of their five-year relationship was taking its toll. It seemed that everything was piling up at once, not just John's personal problems but also the immigration question and the long drawn-out Beatles' settlement.

The drinking and the pain grew steadily worse. John barely knew what

Above: John lived in a friend's house in Bel Air, Los
Angeles, during the last part of 1973 and first half of
1974. He said: "I just went there to get out of New
York for a bit and try to create something to do down
there—but I spent most of the time lying around with
Harry Nilsson and Ringo and people like that,
ending up in the papers! That went on for about nine
months—just one big hangover, it was hell."

Opposite: Back to sanity in the Dakota apartment
overlooking New York's Central Park.

Hanging out in Los Angeles: The only song John wrote during the whole period was the depressive "Nobody Loves You (When You're Down And Out)."

was happening to him. His friends didn't help either; rather, they encouraged him: "When I've been drunk or disembodied in one way or another, there're always friends and hangers-on who sit around applauding as they hand me more and more stuff to kill myself with. It's like Bob Dylan says in that song, 'pull you down in the hole that he's in.' But whenever I say these things, I'm careful not to blame other people."

John had been drinking with Harry Nilsson a lot and one morning he said, "What are we doing? Why don't we do some work instead of just getting into trouble, you know? My name gets into the paper, you never get mentioned and I get all the problems, and *I'm* the one with the immigration problem—so let's do something constructive!"

This suggestion resulted in John's agreeing to produce an album for Nilsson—"Pussycats"—which was an ideal solution, since he was in no mood even to consider making his own record. Thinking he had come up with a brilliant idea, John asked Harry, Ringo, Klaus Voormann—and somehow Keith Moon got in on the act—to all live together, so they would be "in tune." But it turned into another madhouse.

"After the first session," John said, "Harry comes to me and he's got no throat—no voice whatsoever! I don't know whether it was psychological or what. So there I've got this great singer with no voice. . . . I suddenly got sober in the middle of all that. 'I'm responsible, I'm the producer, I'd better straighten out!' I thought." He had to lock himself in his bedroom to keep away from the drinking and succeeded this way in fulfilling his commitment. When the album was finished John felt much better for having worked, a satisfying contrast to the previous months of constant partying.

Tired of waiting for Phil Spector to reappear, John decided the time was right to head back to New York. Armed with only one song written in L.A., a depressing but poignant ballad called "Nobody Loves You (When You're Down and Out)"—"I had been sitting on the song because I knew I would ruin it if I tried to record it at the time I wrote it—my head wasn't together to deal with it so I just kept it in my pocket"—he made plans for a new solo album.

During the last part of August John went into the tenth floor studio of the Record Plant on 44th Street with a handful of the best session musicians around, to lay down "Walls and Bridges." He had written all the other songs in one of his prolific outbursts after returning to the city. His crew was comprised basically of Jim Keltner on drums, Klaus Voormann on bass, Jesse Ed Davis on guitar, and Nicky Hopkins on piano. Driven hard by John, almost to the point of collapse, they finished the whole album in about three or four days.

"Walls and Bridges" evolved from the chaos and drunkenness of Los Angeles. It came bursting out, surprising even John who was depressed that he had not been writing: "Everything was up in the air and it must have been affecting me although you don't know it at the time. You think you're still functioning. You don't realize what is happening to you. You think, 'I'm doing this and I'm doing that,' but I wasn't doing anything. I wasn't writing anything, I only wrote one song during that whole period."

John enjoyed recording "Walls and Bridges." "I'm surprised it wasn't all bluuggghhh—I had the most peculiar year. I'm just glad *something* came out. It's describing the year, in a way, but it's not as sort of schizophrenic as the year really was. I think I got such a shock during that year that the impact hasn't come through. It isn't all on 'Walls and Bridges' though. There's a hint of it there. It has to do with age and God knows what else. But only the surface has been touched on 'Walls and Bridges.' "

Like "John Lennon/Plastic Ono Band," "Walls and Bridges" was a catharsis for John, full of autobiographical references. Several lines in "Scared " sum up the problem, expressing John's anxieties about age creeping up on him and of being alone with "no place to call my own." "I got the title," John explained, "from one of those public service announcements that I'm always watching on TV. I was flicking through the channels as I usually do—and I heard the phrase 'walls and bridges,' and filed it in my head because I liked it. Walls keep you in, either protectively or otherwise, and bridges get you somewhere else. It's sort of poetic, and it says everything without saying anything, and so I kept it." "Whatever Gets You Thru The Night " was John's hit single off the album, and featured his new friend Elton John on organ, piano, and vocals. The song was an upbeat rocker, its title from "whatever gets you thru the night is alright." As John remarked: "You can put it down to which night with which bottle or what night in which town. . . ."

Musically, "Walls and Bridges" was a surprise, almost a relief. Many people expected to hear music as morbid as the subject matter, but it was the reverse. There was pleasure and a vitality in the music that excelled anything John had ever recorded on his own. The dark cloud over his thinking and his creativity had lifted. Able to understand what he had been through, he could feel and think clearly and make good music again. The record was a triumph for John's musical credibility.

The day before he started on "Walls and Bridges," a deal had been made on the L.A. rock 'n' roll tapes, which Phil Spector then sent back to John. Since he couldn't deal with them at that time, John put them aside until the end of the "Walls and Bridges" sessions. Then he pulled them

John with Elton John, who ''sort of zapped in and played the piano and ended up singing 'Whatever Gets You Thru the Night,''' at the Record Plant.

out and listened to the eight tracks. "I didn't even want to hear them, the feelings were so bad about it, but I listened to 'em and only about four were saveable. The rest were all miles out of tune, just mad, you couldn't use 'em. Twenty-eight guys playing out of tune. . . . So I salvaged what there was of 'em and I was getting depressed—what could I do? Make an E.P. [extended play] but they don't have E.P.'s in America. . . . Put them out one by one? I wasn't sure enough of their quality to be a single. Some of them were alright but I didn't feel that confident about 'em. So then I thought, 'oh, I'll record some more.' "

John immediately booked time at the Record Plant and assembled most of the musicians he had used on "Walls and Bridges." With the usual burst of frenetic energy and Lennon as the driving force, ten more songs were recorded in five days. These included "Be-Bop-A-Lula," "Stand By Me," "Ready Teddy," "Rip It Up," "Ain't That A Shame," "Do You Want To Dance," "Slippin' And Slidin'," "Peggy Sue," "Bring It On Home To Me," "Send Me Some Lovin'," and "Ya-Ya."

However, even after these sessions John still felt very insecure about the project: "It started out fun, became hell, and ended up fun, and then I wasn't sure what it was. The ones I did didn't sound like the ones Phil did, and I thought everyone's going to shout at me for putting it out. It was a good idea in '73 and now it's '74 and maybe '75, and they're all going to say 'he shouldn't have done it, why did he do it?' And there was so much build-up waiting for this great record of Lennon-Spector, and I nearly, for the first time ever, didn't put it out.

"Then I let people hear it, people who hadn't been involved, and the record company, and they said: 'it's alright, we like it,' and friends liked it that hadn't been there. So then it went out."

The finished record, simply entitled "John Lennon—Rock 'n' Roll," came out in March 1975. It was an instant success.

John's renewed spirit was revealed when he made a surprise appearance at an Elton John concert. Their relationship had flourished from the moment Elton, in John's words, "sort of popped in on the session for 'Walls and Bridges' and sort of zapped in and played the piano and ended up singing 'Whatever Gets You Thru the Night' with me—which was a great shot in the arm. . . . Then I heard from a friend—'cause he was shy— would I be there when he cut 'Lucy'? Maybe play on it but just be there? So I went along. And I sang in the chorus and contributed the reggae in the middle. And then, again through a mutual friend, he asked if it got to be Number One ['Whatever Gets You Thru the Night'], would I appear onstage with him, and I said sure, not thinkin' in a million years it was gonna get to Number One."

Back at the Dakota in February 1975, John relaxes, happy to be back with Yoko: "We blew apart, we didn't even plan to get back together. I was just gonna visit her, and I'd visited her many times before, and I just walked in and I thought 'I live here, this is my home, here's Yoko, here's me.' The other times I'd visited we'd spent hours together but I hadn't been relaxed. This last time I just never left."

So John made good his promise at Elton John's Thanksgiving Madison Square Garden concert. Word leaked out to the audience that John would appear, and the anticipation built up until it recalled the excitement of Beatlemania. The instant John sprinted out the crowd roared its approval. He looked fantastic in a black cloak, chewing gum as always, his guitar jerking around his neck as he launched into "Whatever Gets You Thru the Night." The crowd was ecstatic. Next John joined Elton for the chorus of "Lucy In The Sky With Diamonds." Lastly, John announced that they would sing "an old Beatles' song we never did on stage: 'I Saw Her Standing There.' " Elton himself was so excited, so happy, and so amazed by what was happening that he was in tears.

John said afterward: "I was moved by it, but everybody else was in *tears*. I felt guilty 'cause I wasn't in tears. I just went up and did a few numbers. But the emotional thing was me and Elton. . . . It was a great high night, a really high night."

The event had a special significance for John not only because of the reception given to him but because Yoko was at the concert, a fact he was unaware of until he came face to face with her backstage: "I didn't know she was there, 'cause if I'd known she was there I'd've been too nervous to go on, you know, I would have been terrified. . . . She was backstage afterward, and there was just that moment when we saw each other and like, it's like in the movies, you know, when time stands still. And there was silence, everything went silent, and we were just sort of lookin' at each other and . . . oh, hello . . . And somebody said, 'Well, there's two people in love.' That was before we got back together. But that's probably when we felt something. It was very weird. . . ."

By the end of 1974 a reconciliation between John and Yoko seemed at least possible. John said: "It's hard to discuss the situation between me and Yoko, because it's so personal and because I'm not quite sure myself. Yoko and I are sort of separated but equal and together. I don't know what else to say except that Yoko is probably the first and only woman I've ever been with who'll remain a real friend, no matter what goes down with our marriage."

And then out of the blue John went back to the apartment in the Dakota on Central Park West, where Yoko had been living alone. Quietly he came home with the papers he had gone out to buy a year earlier, and his only comment to the press was "The separation didn't work out." "It *didn't* work out," he later elaborated, "and the reaction to the breakup was all that madness. I was like a chicken without a head. . . . I feel like

John in front of his jukebox in the Dakota. John and Yoko found the apartment by chance: "We got it by a fluke," John explained. "It's hard to get in the building—it's big and it's beautiful, we've lived here two years already, off and on. We lived in a massive house in England, but we always lived in the bedroom or the kitchen. Then we went to the extreme when we got to New York, we lived in two rooms for eighteen months and that was beginning to get a little much—the Dakota is perfect! I can't see us moving, it's long term."

John on the roof of the Dakota; he has a passion for wearing badges and cowboy boots, but his image now, he thinks, is "pretty normal." "I don't really know what yer image is, it sort of creates itself. I don't live it down; I've played it both ways, especially when you first get money. I had all the biggest cars in the world and I don't even like cars, I've bought everything that I could buy, the only things I never got into was yachts. So I went thru *that* period, and then there's nothin' else to do, once you do it. So I just live however makes me most comfortable."

John and Yoko seen together for the first time in public after their year's separation, at the Grammy Awards presentation. Below left to right: David Bowie, Art Garfunkel, Paul Simon, Yoko, John, and Aretha Franklin.

I've been on Sinbad's voyage, you know, and I've battled all those monsters and I've got back!"

John was simply happy and relieved to be back with Yoko and back in New York instead of lying in some weird place with a hangover. "We got back together because we *love* each other," he emphasized. "Seventy-four was just hell, I mean just a drag! . . . Seventy-four lasted about three years—a little of it tailed into the beginning of seventy-five, but I just feel good now and I'm writing well—and I'm happy!"

STAY ALIVE IN SEVENTY-FIVE

John and Yoko's first public appearance together after their reconciliation was at the Grammy Awards presentation. "I was glad it was big, and it was quick," John said, "so we got maximum effect and it sort of said it without having to go thru a big routine—it just sort of went in all the right papers and magazines, and there we were, and that's it. There's nothing else to say—ha! ha! It's all over! So it's good that I hadn't been seen around before that. At one time I was sort of on practically every TV show all the time and in every newspaper going on about immigration, and people got bored stiff, including me. Then the next bout was being drunk in Los Angeles, so I thought I better keep out of the way a bit. . . . I was going to do the Grammies anyway, because I thought it was about time they saw I was not abnormal and drunk all the time, that I could speak, so I thought it would be a good opportunity to kill two birds with one stone—a) show that sometimes I'm sober, and b) that I was back with my wife and that everything, as far as I was concerned, was back to normal. . . . We knew we were gonna get back together one day, but it could've been ten years—it was fate, so we knew we'd get back together one way or other, but we'd no idea when."

John's fight against deportation proceedings had grown more complex, but everything was at last starting to go in his favor. The names and details of those involved in the illegal conspiracy to kick him out of America were revealed in the December 1974 issue of *Rolling Stone.* Several months earlier John had asked U.S. District Court Judge Richard Owen to let him prove the Watergate connection: "I respectfully urge that the cause of justice will be advanced by permitting me to demonstrate that my case has been selectively prosecuted in a discriminatory manner; that I have been the subject of illegal surveillance activities on the part of the government; that as a result, my case and the various applications filed in my behalf have been prejudged for reasons unrelated to my immigration status," he said in his affidavit.

With much excitement it was announced on January 2, 1975, that Judge Owen had ruled in favor of John, that as they had requested, his lawyers would be permitted to see the Immigration files. The decision, said John's lawyer Leon Wildes, was "a significant step forward in vindicating my client's position that he had been selectively prosecuted because of his anti-administration opinions." The files confirmed everything that had already leaked out, and so in June 1975, John filed suit in Manhattan Federal Court against former attorney general John Mitchell and other government officials. The suit, which also named former attorney general Richard Kleindienst and officials of the Immigration and Naturalization Service, charged that the deportation actions directed against him were improper.

By this time the government was beginning to back down. Federal prosecutor Paul Curran informed Judge Owen that the INS, "without conceding that its previous action was incorrect or irregular, had determined to undertake a review of the question of possible nonpriority status for the plaintiff. . . ." Furthermore, Curran advised, no immigration official who had taken part in the case before would be at all connected with the review.

Yoko had become pregnant at the beginning of the year, and after her previous record of miscarriages John was determined to do everything possible to help her relax and have a perfect pregnancy. She was so fragile that the least upset could cause complications, so John took her to stay in a country house outside New York and all plans were canceled. In late September the Immigration Service granted John a temporary nonpriority status—a kind of bureaucratic limbo—because of the pregnancy. They said that as long as Yoko was pregnant, giving birth or in any stage of postpartum difficulty, they would not kick him out. Nor in any case would they act until the Court of Appeals, which was considering John's case, came to a decision.

On October 7, 1975, the battle was suddenly over when the U.S. Court of Appeals overturned the order to deport John. The decision caught him by surprise; it was not expected for another month and no one had been willing to predict the outcome. The court rendered a thirty-page, at times moving, decision. Not only did it rule against the Immigration and Naturalization Service, it went so far as to call John a patriot: "If, in our 200 years of independence, we have in some measure realized our ideals, it is in large part because we have always found a place for those committed to the spirit of liberty and willing to implement it," the court wrote in its two-to-one decision. "Lennon's four-year battle to remain in our country is testimony to his faith in this American dream." The

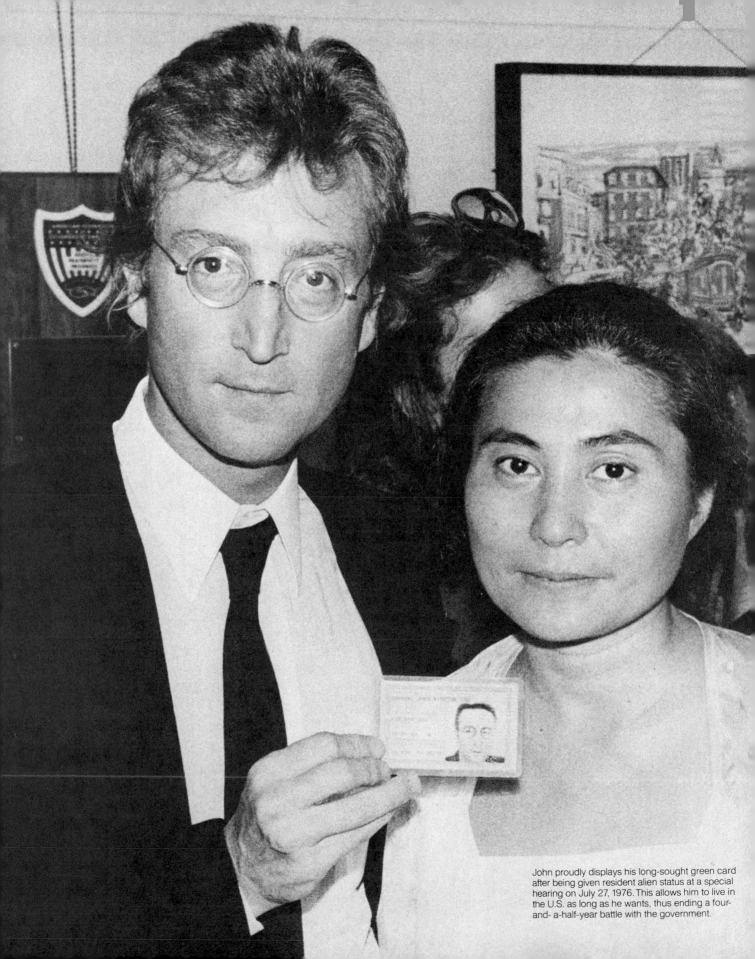

John proudly displays his long-sought green card after being given resident alien status at a special hearing on July 27, 1976. This allows him to live in the U.S. as long as he wants, thus ending a four- and- a-half-year battle with the government.

Immigration authorities had said that John was not eligible for permanent residency because of his marijuana conviction in England. The Court of Appeals ruled that the British law under which John had been convicted was unjust by U.S. standards, and that therefore he had been denied due process by U.S. standards.

Two days after the court's decision—on John's birthday—Yoko gave birth to Sean Ono Lennon, a healthy eight-pound ten-ounce boy, in New York Hospital. After so many sad experiences in the past, having the baby was the most exciting and positive thing that could have happened to John and Yoko. They had both wanted it so much that to them the birth was really something of a miracle. ''I feel as high as the Empire State Building,'' said an ecstatic John.

To celebrate these two momentous events, John put out ''Shaved Fish,'' a collection of all his best songs going back to 1969. It was a strong concept album in the sense that for the first time all these songs could be considered as a whole. Before, half of them had been available only as singles. The essence of John's best work was here—from ''Give Peace A Chance'' through ''Power to the People'' to ''Woman Is the Nigger of the World,'' from ''Imagine'' to ''Mind Games'' and ''Whatever Gets You Thru the Night,'' and from the earlier period, ''Cold Turkey'' and ''Instant Karma.'' Together these songs revealed the power and intensity of John's music.

The Dakota building on Central Park West.

Recently, both John and Yoko have had more time to relax and take care of themselves. In the spring of 1976 they went on a forty-day fast, drinking only juices, and now they diet regularly. They've both successfully given up smoking and John even managed to give up sugar. He has enjoyed staying at home, playing the proud father, watching Sean learn to crawl, and pushing the baby carriage in Central Park.

Sadly, John is still harassed by lawsuits and his only time away from the Dakota seems to be taken up by court appearances. His fighting spirit, however, is in no way dampened, and not long ago he won a case (involving the *Rock 'n' Roll* album) in which Morris Levy of Roulette Records was trying to collect forty-two million dollars. After his victory, John said: ''The reason I fought this was to discourage ridiculous suits like this. They didn't think I'd show or that I'd fight it. They thought I'd just settle, but I won't!''

Today John's ties with the past still exist. His relationship with Paul McCartney is now better than it has been since they went their separate ways: ''He visits me every time he's in New York, like all the other rock 'n' roll creeps. I just happen to be the one in New York and I love it, but then they all come down and I'm supposed to show 'em a good time. I don't know what to do with them, but actually they don't want a good time, they just like sitting in rooms like everybody else. So whenever he's in town I see him. He comes over and we just sit around and get mildly drunk and reminisce!"

John also tries to spend as much time as he can with Julian, his twelve-year-old son from his first marriage: "Seeing him is good. I don't see him that often, just on school holidays. We usually talk about once a week on the phone. I can't go to England so he has to come here. I went through a period of 'what are we gonna do?' But then I realized it doesn't really matter, as long as he's around. He grooves in the studio or Disneyland, or whatever you wanna do. I didn't know that till I found out!"

It must be hell, John thinks, having John Lennon for a father. "He's a Beatle fan but I think he likes Paul better than me. He's a bright kid and he's into music—and I didn't encourage him. He's already got a band in school; it's embarrassing, but they sing old rock 'n' roll songs 'cause their teacher is my age. He even turns me on to new groups! I call him up and say 'have you seen *Sparks?* They've got Hitler on the piano,' and he says, 'no, they're all right, but have you seen *Queen?*' Their age group is hipper to music."

John's fight to remain in the United States finally came to an end on July 27, 1976, when his application to become a permanent resident was formally approved at a special hearing before immigration judge Ira Fieldsteel. During the one-hour hearing the judge heard testimony praising John's character and value as a resident. Gloria Swanson, Norman Mailer, Geraldo Rivera, and sculptor Isamu Noguchi all came to his defense, describing him as a generous and public-minded person as well as an important artist to welcome to the American music scene. The Immigration Service lawyer said the Government no longer objected to John's presence here, and Mr. Fieldsteel awarded John his long-awaited green card—No. A 17-597-321. "It's great to be legal again," John said with relief, as he hugged and kissed Yoko.

PART TWO

THE MAGIC

THE PRIMITIVE MUSICIAN

"When I first heard music I was transfixed. I didn't think about it, I just fell in love with music. I was completely hypnotized . . . the real Pied Piper was rock 'n' roll. When I first heard it I dropped everything else."   (John Lennon, 1974)

John woke up one morning ecstatic, bubbling with excitement and shouting like a kid because he had a great new tune in his head. He was totally absorbed in it when I took breakfast upstairs and already the lyrics seemed to be pouring out of him: "Instant Karma's gonna knock you right on the head, get yourself together you're gonna be dead."

I sensed John's energy level rising as he glanced at me with that familiar twinkle in his eyes, a happy satisfied look which he always had when he was creating. Before I had time to put the breakfast tray down he leapt out of bed, still in his white bathrobe, and stormed downstairs straight to the upright piano in the kitchen. Singing the basic melody line over and over again, he hammered out chords, trying to find the best sequence. I felt the song take shape almost immediately, the music flowing from him, as he scribbled the words on a small sheet of paper. The message echoed around the kitchen walls as his voice rose to a primitive crescendo: "Why are we here? . . . not to live in pain and fear, you're ev'rywhere—get your share."

After half an hour of sipping tea and working at the song John decided he wanted to go to the studio and record it right away; he was impatient and there was an urgency in his manner. "Let's get going!" he shouted as he ran back upstairs to get dressed and hurry Yoko up. I called Les and asked him to have the car outside in five minutes.

In the back of the Mercedes John relaxed and thought about how he wanted "Instant Karma" to sound, at the same time working on a new verse. He wanted a very basic rock 'n' roll sound that would come over well on the radio, and suddenly came up with an idea: "Spector! Let's get Phil Spector in on the session, he'll get the sound I want!" (Allen Klein had brought Spector to London hoping that he might be able to "produce the Beatles," and as a trial run they had given him the chaotic tapes of "Let it Be" to see if he could make a record out of them.)

As we approached the outskirts of London John realized that there was no piano in our office at Apple and he needed one desperately to finish the song when we arrived. "Well, we'll just pick one up on the way in," he said, and asked Les to stop at one of the big music stores. In the center of the city, not far from Apple, we pulled up outside Imhoff's. After staring out the car window for a few seconds John chose the best looking piano from the storefront display and instructed Les to go in, buy it, and arrange for it to be delivered to Apple as fast as possible.

We raced up the steps past the Apple scruffs and on into the office. John and Yoko sat down behind their desk. Yoko began opening the mail while I buzzed the kitchen for hot tea and vegetables. John couldn't concentrate on anything but the new song and he set about deciding which musicians he would use. He asked me to call E.M.I. Studios to book time starting at six and then to locate Phil Spector, Klaus Voormann and Alan White. Spector was easy to find as he was ensconced in his suite at the Inn on the Park Hotel, and the others were tracked down after a series of phone calls.

A moment later I glanced through the two-way mirrored office door and saw the piano being wheeled into reception. The power of a Beatle still worked miracles, I thought to myself. John couldn't wait to get at it. The piano was barely in position when he pulled up the plush green stool and started work on the nearly completed chorus. He sang it through several times trying to find the right pace: "we all shine on like the moon and the stars and the sun, we all shine on, on and on!"

Quick to respond to John's invitation, Phil Spector was the next to arrive, exuding energy as he bounced into the room with his two bodyguards close behind him. But he appeared a little nervous, so John beckoned him to the piano and launched right into the song. There was immediate communication; Spector understood exactly how John wanted it to sound. George Harrison shot in and out of the room, staying just long enough to sense the excitement from John and Phil, to listen to the song, and to agree to play on the session later.

By seven that evening everyone was assembled in Studio One at E.M.I. Kevin and Mal, the roadies, had all the mikes and instruments set up. Spector was running around like a wild man fiddling with the knobs of the control board, and John was shouting impatiently, "O.K. 'Instant Karma' Take One!"

Several hours later, after working out all the instrumentation, experiment-

"Rock 'n' roll music gets right through to you without having to go through your brain," John said. "Rock 'n' roll music goes right to the gut!"

ing with vocals, and listening to several playbacks, John decided that he wanted a lot of voices for the chorus. Instead of trying to get a group of vocalists together at that late hour he sent Kevin and Mal out to the nearest nightclub to gather carloads of any kids who were in the mood for singing. They were soon back with a motley bunch from "Speakeasy," and George took it upon himself to act as choirmaster, explaining the chorus and conducting.

John was ready with his vocal now, and to the forceful beat of Alan White's drumming he proceeded to lay down a scalding delivery of the song. The intensity in his face was accentuated by his short hair, so recently cropped off during the turmoil in Denmark. I thought of the aborted Peace Festival and all the related craziness which had gone down just a few weeks before as his searing voice cut through the line: "How are you gonna see laughin' at fools like me."

After recording several takes with the "choir" which now included just about anyone around who wasn't playing an instrument, John and Spector felt confident that it was "in the can."

Afterwards, John was physically and emotionally drained but he felt high, really elated at having succeeded in translating his conception of a song into a finished record in less than twelve hours. But this was typical of John's impassioned methods. He knew no other way of tackling his work and accomplished everything he did through this supercharged energy. Conversely, in a flash his energy might also subside, for it was part of a larger interlocking cycle which made up the pace of John's life. This instinct for pace, the innate knowledge of when to wait, when to push on, when to turn aside, is one of his best characteristics.

"Instant Karma," released a week after the recording session in February 1970, and "Cold Turkey," the Plastic Ono Band's single before that, were the beginning of John's evolution away from the Beatles. But more important they were a way back to his roots, reuniting him with his earliest musical feelings. It was a torrent of energy that John poured into the production of "Cold Turkey," with its powerful ferocious vocal, as if he had been locked up and constrained for years, then suddenly let out and allowed to sing for only five minutes. It was basically primitive. Both these songs showed a return to the driving inspiration that had kicked off John's musical career, way before the Beatles had started—*primitive rock 'n' roll.*

"I was constantly making up music," John said, "playing mouth organs, accordions, piano, anything I could lay my hands on as a kid. I sang and

John was deeply influenced by Yoko's experimentation with avant-garde voice techniques.

imitated others, but the real Pied Piper was rock 'n' roll. When I heard it I dropped everything else. It was instinctive. Rock 'n' roll music gets right through to you without having to go through your brain. Rock 'n' roll music goes right to the gut!''

John possesses one of *the* archetypal rock 'n' roll voices—raw, aggressive and ultimately primitive. His howling rock bombardments have been his tour de force ever since the Cavern days of "Twist and Shout" and "Money." But after so many years in the studio with the Beatles he began to hold back, repressing the intensity and spontaneity of performing live: "It used to get a bit embarrassing in front of George or Paul because we knew each other so well . . . Oh! He's trying to be Elvis; Oh! He's doing this now. We were a bit supercritical of each other, so we inhibited each other a lot."*

With Yoko's help and by her example, these inhibitions were swept away. John was deeply influenced by the avant-garde voice techniques she had experimented with, and he was fascinated with her ability to use her vocal cords like an instrument. In "Cold Turkey" the looseness of John's vocal style adds a ferocious power to the song, accentuating the equally potent words. And on his first solo album John was able to use this regained vocal freedom to match the painful and traumatic subject matter of the songs.

"Basically I'm what I call a primitive musician," John has said, "meaning no schooling—didn't ever take the instrument that far, just took it far enough to enable me to do what I wanted to do, which was express myself . . . I put it as primitive, like those primitive painters—that's how I look upon me songs and the music I make personally."

I always felt that John's primitiveness was synonymous with the pain and loneliness of his childhood and the resulting intense urge for self-expression. His natural longing for love and companionship remained unfulfilled and became a lifelong craving which periodically found ecstatic release in his music. The frankness, the unrestrained compulsion to confide, to lay himself bare, and the intensity of John's thoughts created a style which is direct and effective, honest and alive. And in the shadow of bitterness and frustration, John is struggling for his existence, surviving only by this power to reveal himself.

Continuing the analogy with primitive painters John said: "Just like Van Gogh was, or any of those people . . . I'm interested in expressing myself like they expressed it, in some way that will mean something to people in any country, in any language, and at any time in history."*

Vincent Van Gogh during his lifetime was concerned with the same ambi-

*Lennon Remembers: The Rolling Stone Interviews, Straight Arrow Books, San Francisco, 1971.

John essentially creates his music not from any formal musical background, but from instinct, from his feelings.

tion. He wrote: "Yes, here in my head, behind the walls of my brain, great things reside. I shall be able to give something to the world, which perhaps will keep people concerned for a century and which perhaps will require a century to think about."

Lennon and Van Gogh are both artists with an innate inner vision who have led eventful and agitated private lives. They both created out of pain. And they have shared the common themes of hope and failure, love and loneliness, their life dramas touching moments of sensationalism. But Van Gogh encountered only wounding rejection during his lifetime and his final despair led to suicide. John, though he goes through fits of depression and has felt that same rejection, is a survivor, not a suicidal type. But both create from their own perceptions: Van Gogh said in 1885 that "the real painters do not paint things as they are, after a dry and learned analysis. They paint them as *they themselves* feel them to be." So John essentially creates his music not from any formal musical background but from instinct, from his feelings.

Artists discover all the time that it doesn't matter how you approach your work, you will always come back to your own self and your own obsessive themes. Salvador Dali has spoken about the obsessive mania of the artist, saying in essence that an artist is really no good unless he is possessed, but they are both artists who are in the grip of something bigger than themselves. Dali presents his haunting box of surreal images and John gives us his primitive transfusion of sounds shooting ambivalent messages into our collective subconscious.

John's magic, his musical metamorphosis, is a phenomenon that continually surprises me. The creation of "Instant Karma" was one example. Also incised in my memory was John's transformation at the Toronto Rock 'n' Roll Revival, when I saw a pathetic figure of a man, crying, throwing up, and convulsed with fear, who walked out onto a stage and gave an inspired performance.

This ability to create out of pain has been a constant background to John's career. His continual life drama, the special character of his proximity to tragedy goes along with the will power to unify through music the disparate aspects of personality. In the song "Intuition," on the "Mind Games" album, John tells us that when he struggles in the night it's the magic of the music that shows him the way, and in the song "#9 Dream" he sings of music touching his soul. John's confrontation with pain and the authority with which he tackles it is provocative and forces a response from the listener, making it hard to ignore such lines as "Please help me, I'm drowning in a sea of hatred. . . ."

John goes through constant transformations. His experience is never static, and out of this ever changing interior world comes the all-important growth so crucial to an artist. John's music imitates his stutterings, fumblings and awkward silences—his songs have been a barometer of his life. But his talent transforms life; the music transcends reality.

Out of his love for Yoko, John distilled the essence of their relationship, creating a series of melodic and poignant love songs far removed from his usual catalog. John can instinctively compose music evocative of love, and the nurturing that leads to its fulfillment, as easily as he can cough up the hieroglyphics of pain. He has always been a great accommodator of opposites. And it is this capacity to keep in mind two antithetical points of view that gives tautness and unpredictability to his work. He has also been able to capture his own emotions and feelings at the *critical moments* in his life and relationships. John has this capacity to share his flaws with his public. He is able to reveal to us the tangled chords of John Lennon, registering only the essences of rock-bottom emotion.

THE
POET AND
PAINTER

IN HIS OWN WRITE

The night of June 18, 1968 it was raining and as the taxi screeched to a halt outside the National Theatre I could see the cream of London society running for cover and terrified of getting their best evening clothes wet. Swarms of them flowed out of chauffeur-driven Rolls Royces and Bentleys to attend a special performance of the play *In His Own Write*, which was based on John's two books, one also titled *In His Own Write* and the other called *Spaniard in the Works*. Originally entitled *Act 1, Scene 3*, the play had been adapted from the books by Adrienne Kennedy, an American dramatist, and the actor Victor Spinetti, and had been tried out the previous summer at a Sunday experimental evening at the National Theatre. Sir Laurence Olivier had liked it sufficiently to insist that it be put into the regular repertoire.

Government censorship in the personage of the Lord Chamberlain predictably hacked up the play: everything that was either blasphemous or derogatory to the Establishment had to go. The fact that the books had been for sale in bookstores for three years made no difference. You could read anti-Establishment literature, but you couldn't put it on the stage. So, for example, a mock TV vicar had to be cut because he gave an Epilogue during which he called upon Almighty Griff. And what remained threw the drama critics into confusion.

"In came a small, angularce man," it went. "We stood astoundergast." Topical delights included references to Pregnant de Gaulle, Sir Alice Doubtless-Whom and Rockall and Fredastaire. The leading character is called Me, a lad born, like John, on October 9, 1940. His family is anchored around the television, hypnotized by the never-ending flicker. The radio and the comics in his bedroom take him into fantasies about the jungle and Sherlock Holmes. School outings to incomprehensible Shakespeare plays, giant cowboys looming over him at the movies, gibberish mumbled in church, pointless and witless discussions on late night

TV—all these affect Me as they have affected all youth. But Me is left amazed and laughing quietly to himself, the eternal outsider.

John arrived at the First Night performance with Yoko, and their entrance, fifteen minutes late, caused a loud stir in the audience. After the play John was surrounded by reporters and cameramen, but they were only interested in one question: "Where is your wife?" No questions about his writing or the play. It was one of his first public appearances with Yoko and the press used it to attack him the next day on the front pages.

In His Own Write provided us with a picture of our times, seen through John's own distorting mirror. It is the joking of a desperate and original mind who really thinks there's nothing much to laugh at anymore. "I was bored when the nasties were still booming us." The language stemmed from John's refusal to speak the smug talk of an unquestioning adult world, and demonstrated his growing bitterness toward the people who used to surround him. The play's concern was for the terrible frustration of adolescence, when all sorts of new things happened in your head and there never seemed to be anybody around to explain them to you. It took a savage swipe at the influences that claim dominance over us— newspapers, radio, and TV—and it pointed out how we are brainwashed by all these things before we go out into the world.

The play also showed a mind holding onto the innocence and wonder of childhood while reaching for awareness and refusing to be buried. It demonstrated an eternal but in this case particularly violent conflict, in which words become an articulated revenge against a hostile world. Rejection of the adult world and escape into a private one were both symbolized in a private language that had its origin in John's earlier poems and drawings. Four legged things are everywhere in the two books— sheep, cats, cows, and Sherlock Holmes on his knees. In the first book there is a huge Wrestling Dog ("but who would fight this wondrous beast? I wouldn't for a kick off"), and a piece called Liddypool which is accompanied by a sketch of chatting quadropuses. Animals and freaks have a certain comic dignity while adults, bent over and crawling, appear silly and too big. The implication is that adults *are* silly since they give their children rubbish to read and expect them to like it.

Docker Adenoid appears along with Harassed MacMillion and the late Cassandle of the Mirror on the Wall. "Vile ruperts" spread through a village; an old man leaves his "last will and testicle." A special day is a "red lettuce day." The whole world shrinks to the nonsense one of a book for small children. Its so-called morality is seen by "old leather lungs," as George Harrison's mother used to describe him, as riddled with evil. Eric

John and Yoko arrive at the opening night of the National Theatre's production of his *In His Own Write,* June 18, 1968.

Opposite: The poem John created as the introduction to his set of Erotic Lithographs, *Bag One.* He etched the poem directly onto a zinc plate in the Curwen Studio atelier, London, in February, 1969.

A is for Parrot which we can plainly see.

B is for glasses which we can plainly see.

C is for plastic which we can plainly see

D is for Doris

E is for binoculars I'll get it in five

F is for Ethel who lives next door

G is for Orange which we love to eat when we can get them because they come from abroad.

H is for England and (Heather)

I is for monkey we see in the tree

J is for parrot which we can plainly see.

K is for shoe top we wear to the ball

L is for lamo because brown

M is for Venezuela where the oranges come from

N is for Brazil near Venezuela (very near)

O is for football which we kick about a bit

T is for Tommy who won the war

Q is a garden which we can plainly see

R is for intestines which hurt when we dance

S is for pancake or whole wheat bread

U is for Ethel who lives on the hill

P is arabs and her sister will

V is for me

W is for lighter which never lights

X is easter — have one yourself

Y is a crooked letter and you can't straighten it

Z is for Apple which we can plainly see.

This is my story both humble and true
take it to pieces and mend it with glue.

John Lennon 1969. Feb.

Hearble, who has a growth on his head, loses his job teaching spastics to dance ("'We're not having a cripple teaching our lads,' said Headmaster"). Randolph, who had to spend Christmas alone, is slaughtered by his pals—"at least he didn't *die* alone, did he?"

So John described his private reaction to the society into which he had been born. Critics of the daily tabloid dismissed the piece as the culmination of "a century of British rubbish," completely failing to notice the aching significance of the play, or John's original books.

THE EROTIC LITHOGRAPHS

"We had some bad scenes earlier this year [the Beatles], so from now on we're determined to be ourselves, open to whatever new influences come along. Perhaps I'll get interested in drawing and painting again. You can't stand still and I think I've been standing still for a bit too long."   (John Lennon, 1969)

It was easy for John to talk about being receptive to new ideas but the discipline to begin projects and see them through to completion was often another story. When in 1968 I suggested the lithographs, John, like I, had no idea that the project would become such an involved and drawn out affair. It was not until over a year later that the lithographs were finally published, and a second set based on the Chinese *I Ching* symbols were never completed.

I kept in touch with John and Yoko after the Coventry Acorn Event, but the first attempts I made to interest John in lithography met with only a vague, distant response. The technicalities of the process seemed alien to him, accustomed as he was to the spontaneity and simplicity of cartoon drawing. John had always considered basic drawing, doodling and sketching his forte, as they best suited his impulsive creative methods; he liked to translate the image from his head to the paper as rapidly as possible and with the least amount of fuss. Often his drawing, like his rhetoric, could not keep pace with his meteoric rush of ideas.

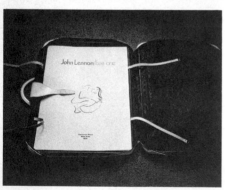

The stylish Italian white leather carrying bag created for each of the three hundred sets of Erotic Lithographs, complete with zips, handles, and a lock. The title *Bag One* and John's signature are imprinted on the side of the bag (top). The open bag displaying the frontispiece to *John Lennon Bag One* (bottom).

Opposite: John's lithograph of himself and Yoko on their honeymoon in Paris.

John was slightly more enthusiastic about the project when, with the help of publisher Ed Newman and the Curwen Studio, I devised a way to shortcut the complicated procedure of working directly onto stone blocks or zinc plates. By using specially treated "litho paper," which I had sent out to his house along with an array of suitable brushes, litho ink, and crayons, John would be able to draw or paint in his usual manner. The images could later be transferred from the paper onto sensitized zinc plates by means of an advanced technical process, and the lithographs printed in the traditional way.

Nothing was heard from John for three or four months after the materials

John's lithograph of the wedding ceremony in Gibraltar in the local magistrate's office.

were sent to him. I had all but given up, certain that they were lying forgotten in some dark closet. But several weeks later after John and Yoko had returned to England from their wedding and the Amsterdam Bed-In I had a phone call from Yoko. John had taken the litho paper with him, had made a series of drawings of the marriage and honeymoon, and was now anxious to see how they would look as lithographs.

The collection of work that I later picked up from John was a veritable potpourri of paintings, ink line drawings, cartoons, and doodles. Yoko was the main subject, there were many portraits and nudes of her. There were also a few evocative ink sketches of scenes such as the wedding ceremony, the two of them walking together in Paris, and an impressionistic rendering of the Bed-In. Ed Newman and I selected four images, which when printed would give John a good indication of the versatility of the translation process from litho paper to actual lithograph.

About this time I started to work for John and Yoko in their office at Apple. The peace campaign was in full swing and John's energy was divided among many commitments in addition to his main priorities of making music and selling peace. It took several months to just schedule a meeting for Newman to bring in the four proofed lithographs, but finally a time was arranged. Ed came into Apple and carefully laid out the prints on John and Yoko's desk. When he saw them John was ecstatic, oohing and ahhing with childlike enthusiasm, laughing, wildly gesticulating and obviously impressed at the results. He seemed thrilled by the new dimension his drawings had taken on, master-printed on the thick luxurious Arches paper. Yoko, too, was excited for John and watched his exuberance with a kind of motherly pride.

This first stage was an obvious success as far as John was concerned, and the question now was where to go from here. I was anxious to see whether he would actually commit himself to have a portfolio published, and what he would want to put in it. Within a couple of minutes John had decided very definitely—yes, he did want his lithographs published and he had already thought up a title for the set: "Bag One." He wanted to do more drawings of Yoko, he explained, and he thought the set would be basically of her and possibly some scenes of them together. Ed Newman brought up the business side of things and it was agreed that he would be the copublisher with John and Yoko's own company, Bag Productions. Newman, however, would arrange all the details and distribution since his New York associates, Consolidated Fine Arts, were one of the biggest lithograph distributors in the United States. Newman himself had a considerable reputation, having already worked with Man Ray, Salvador Dali, Henry Moore and many other prominent European

John's lithograph of the Amsterdam Bed-In.

artists. The meeting ended with John agreeing to start work on the new series of litho drawings as soon as he had time.

But the thrill of the moment passed quickly and the lithographs took on a nonpriority status. The summer of 1969 went by in a series of complex events. By September, John was drawing again but he seemed reluctant to discuss the work at all; an aura of mystery surrounded the project that reminded me of the initial secrecy of the Acorn Event. John's attitude seemed to me to be partly a game and partly just insecurity. However, when I finally got to see the new images I understood why he had been a little hesitant: they were a series of totally intimate drawings that depicted John and Yoko in various acts of love. They were smaller and more detailed than his earlier sketches and I was impressed with their vitality, their simplicity of line, and especially the overall quality of the work. John's draftsmanship had improved considerably since his first efforts.

I felt that the best of this erotic series could be combined with some earlier drawings of the marriage and honeymoon, in order to create an interesting and workable portfolio. John had thought along these lines himself and he was excited when Ed Newman and I started to work out ideas for packaging the lithographs and planning possible exhibitions in London, Paris, and New York.

Twelve images were selected for the final set of lithographs, half from the erotic set and half from the original drawings. John gave Ed Newman and myself carte blanche to make the choice and we picked the most vibrant images that would work together to create an interesting thematic collection. For the printing of the lithographs Newman wanted the very best quality and our first choice took us to Paris to visit the famed masterlithographers, the Crommylynck Brothers, who were Picasso's personal printmakers. Their tiny atelier was crammed with erotic etchings from a book they were working on with Picasso. Aldo Crommylynck, the tall distinguished looking brother, was the spokesman and he agreed to proof two of John's lithographs to show us the results they could get. The only problem was that he didn't know when they would have time to schedule printing the whole edition, as they had such a backlog of work for Picasso—who apparently might call them at any moment to go to the south of France to work on new etchings at his house.

Before I left Paris I had a meeting with Salvador Dali, who was anxious to work with John on some incredible project. (John never seemed interested in Dali's many attempts to get together with him.) Dali was an amazing character; it was useless trying to follow what he said as he spoke his own concoction of Spanish, French and English all mixed together—the result, as I think he intended, was totally incomprehen-

A simple, evocative study of Yoko, one of John's Erotic Lithographs.

sible. His butler served tea and at the end of my "audience" he proceeded to make an object for me to take back to John. Using anything at hand—flowers, napkins, makeup—Dali created a surreal bouquet with a strange face painted on top of it; finally he squeezed a tube of gold liquid paint to create a message for John and signed his name with an elaborate flourish. As I left his suite at the Meurice I wondered how he could still have such incredible energy—he was surely in his eighties.

When the two proofed lithographs arrived from the Crommylyncks they were beautiful, both printed in brown sepia. But the snag was the time factor—they had decided that they definitely wouldn't be able to start on John's sets for at least six months due to the heavy demands of Picasso. That was too long to wait and we decided to let the Curwen Studio take on the project—they had proofed John's original four prints and their atelier was by far the best in London.

John became more involved, in his on and off way, and came to visit the Curwen Studio to see the printing process in action. While there, he created the image for the frontispiece, a simple sketch of himself crouched on the ground holding Yoko, which he drew directly onto a zinc plate. John was fascinated by the huge Heidelberg presses and watched intently as one of his own plates was put on for proofing. He had written a long alphabet poem, beginning "A is for parrot which we can clearly see," as an introduction to the portfolio, and he laboriously copied it out onto another zinc plate so that the poem itself would become a lithograph. This brought the total number of prints in the set up to fourteen, and the edition was to be limited to three hundred sets.

The packaging of Bag One was of prime importance in bringing a cohesive feeling to the whole project. John had already agreed that a specially designed bag would be the obvious solution. So Ed Newman commissioned Ted Lapidus, the French clothes designer, to create a stylish white carrying bag complete with zips, handles and a lock. Three hundred leather bags, each to hold a complete set of lithographs, were hand-stitched by craftsmen in Italy. As a final touch to the creation, the title Bag One and John's signature were imprinted in black letters onto the white leather.

By the time the lithographs were printed and ready to be signed John had become engrossed in his peace activities again and had very little spare time. In December 1969 he and Yoko were planning their trip to Canada to arrange the peace festival and possibly meet with Prime Minister Trudeau. As the lithographs were to be distributed mainly in America it seemed a good idea for John to sign them while he was in Canada. He had to sign every one of the three thousand prints.

John signs every one of his three thousand lithographs at the Hawkin's farmhouse outside Toronto, as Anthony Fawcett and Ed Newman lend a hand.

Scotland Yard police raid John's exhibition of Erotic Lithographs at the London Arts Gallery and confiscate eight prints.

The location for the signing was Canadian rockabilly singer Ronnie Hawkins' rustic farmhouse outside Toronto. John and Yoko were hiding out there waiting for news of the meeting with Trudeau. The lithographs, which had been shipped to New York, were driven to Toronto by truck. They were held up at the border for twenty-four hours while officials impounded them as possibly obscene, until the publisher's lawyers managed to prove that they were original Fine Arts prints. They finally arrived in the middle of a snowstorm and were stacked up in the living room. It was a surreal sight to see the piles of lithographs almost reaching the ceiling. I wondered whether John would have second thoughts at having to sign every one, but he seemed happy and joked about it.

Ed Newman flew in to supervise the signing. When the time came John set to work and with the help of Ed and myself the signing progressed at quite a speed. John methodically scrawled his name over and over again while we made a kind of human conveyor belt, lifting each lithograph and passing it down the line to its allotted space. This was accomplished with the help of endless cups of tea, many joints, and occasional entertainment from Ronnie, who played us his new album of rock 'n' roll songs. John enjoyed the entire two days' work, and in between signing bouts we all rode Ski-Doos and Amphicats at high speed around the snow-covered fields.

Bag One, the Erotic Lithographs, were now ready to be seen. The first exhibition of the set was at the London Arts Gallery, in January 1970. John could not come to the opening because he and Yoko were staying in the north of Denmark with Kyoko and Tony Cox. The lithographs were on sale for forty pounds each or five hundred and fifty pounds for the set. Inevitably, on the second day of the exhibition, the police raided the gallery with a warrant, supposedly after Scotland Yard had received complaints, and eight of the lithographs were confiscated. The summons alleged that the gallery had "exhibited to public view eight indecent prints to the annoyance of passengers, contrary to Section 54(12) of the Metropolitan Police Act, 1839, and the third schedule of the Criminal Justice Act 1967."

When the case came to court several months later, a Picasso lithograph and a catalog of Picasso drawings were produced at Marlborough Street Magistrates' Court for comparison with John's prints. Detective-Inspector Patrick Luff, of the Central Office, New Scotland Yard, said that when he went to the gallery on January 15 about forty people were viewing the prints. "I saw no display of annoyance from the younger age group, but one gentleman was clearly annoyed," he said. Mr. St. John Harmsworth, the magistrate, asked: "Did he stamp his foot?" "Anger was registered on his face," Inspector Luff replied. Mr. Napley, the defending lawyer, handed over a set of lithographs to the court with the comment: "I hope the officer will not mark them, because no doubt by the end of this case they will be worth more than five hundred and fifty pounds." The case was dismissed when the magistrate decided that John's prints were "unlikely to deprave or corrupt."

The American opening of Bag One was a lavish affair at the Lee Nordness Gallery in New York. I flew over on John's behalf to film the proceedings. The whole of the New York art scene and all the "beautiful people" turned out. Dali came with his pet ocelot on a leash. The lithographs were on view in a specially created environment, where spectators were asked to remove their shoes. The next month's issue of the prestigious *Avant Garde* magazine featured the Erotic Lithographs on the cover and as the major inside spread.

John began work on a new series of prints based on symbols from the Chinese *I Ching* book of proverbs, but he lost interest after the first two were proofed. The series was to have been a joint collaboration between him and Yoko, with John painting the geometric I Ching symbol which he had chosen (such as "communication") and Yoko painting the Japanese equivalent, using her talent for calligraphy. They had both relied heavily on the *I Ching* book at various periods to help them with important decisions. The package of lithographs was going to include a "John and Yoko" edition of the book, with specially minted coins with their heads on each side. The whole affair would have been outrageously commercial, and it is probably best that they never completed it.

An *I Ching* lithograph, the combined effort of John and Yoko. The series was never completed after the first three had been proofed.

THE HERALDIC JOURNEY

"As soon as you've clutched onto something, you think—you're always clutchin' at straws—*this is what life is all about.* I think artists are lucky because the straws are always blowin' out of their hands. But the unfortunate thing is that most people find the straw hat and hang on to it . . . I think I found out it's a waste of time. There is no hat to wear. Just keep moving around and changing clothes is the best. That's all that goes on: *change.*"   (John Lennon, 1975)

John Lennon, the poet and the musician, swings between a passionate welcome to life and furious revulsion against it. He has tried through his music to make people *aware* of their own potentialities, revealing the pathways for growth and exposing the destructive forces that impede growth. Throughout John's heraldic journey it has been his restless spirit which has infused his creativity with its boundless energy.

By the very nature of his personality, John is an artist constantly in a state of flux, always moving on and leaving the debris of his cluttered world behind him. When I walked into his famed arena I saw him as a man hiding behind a series of masks; it was hard to know what lay beneath the aggressive exterior. But I began to piece together his elusive character the first time I visited Kenwood, John's labyrinthine old house. This strange mock-Tudor edifice had sheltered him through the turbulent Beatle years and although the house was being evacuated I felt his presence everywhere. Even in the furthest corners were the pungent relics of a frenzied creativity. In the tiny attic where John had put together many of his favorite songs, the eight Brunel tape recorders were still hooked up, ominously encircling the cramped space. Instruments lay scattered across the floor and an Edwardian circus poster, the inspiration for "Mr. Kite," graced the only wall space. The bedroom was empty. All that remained was an enormous closet full of John's clothes—black velvet frock coats edged in gold braid, pin stripe suits and waistcoats, multicolored satin outfits that were Sgt. Pepper originals, collarless Beatle leftovers, military tunics, and countless army surplus jackets. They told the story of his life, but were now discarded and long forgotten. Left in the cavernous living room were two oversize speakers and a floor-to-ceiling record collection, mainly rock 'n' roll oldies. White-label acetates, unreleased gems from "Let It Be," gathered dust on a turntable.

Gradually, as I spent more time around John, I began to know him, to recognize and anticipate his complex behavior. It was difficult, for there was always a distance, an aloofness, the conscious acting-out of a role. I noticed this directed not only toward myself but to everyone that he came in contact with, except of course for Yoko. At times Yoko would merge into the same identical mold as John, reflecting his feelings, his look, his very expressions. When I talked to them I often had the strange sensation that I was talking to just one person.

John's moods were impossible. He would change from child to clown to guru within the space of minutes, totally at ease with each role. And he was impulsive, his mind raced ahead of his actions. Conversations turned into inarticulate ramblings as vocal cords and ideas tried to synchronize. His stamina was incredible and I often felt that he was asking too much of himself, pushing himself too far. "Discomfort is proper to the poet," wrote Cocteau, "his universe is almost uninhabitable. People sense this. They come into it as little as possible, as quickly as possible and only through curiosity."

I feel that John's greatest musical achievement has been the synthesis of past, present and future, of inner and outer. From his own pain and conflict he has created a musical fusion that reveals the quintessential man. "I'm always at it," John says, "the best stuff always comes out on impulse, or inspiration, and I hardly have to think about it. But I'm always writing, either in the back of my head, or if somebody says something I'm storing it away for a line or an idea, so there's never a moment when I'm not writing, almost. . .I like it when I get the words, then the music just comes—the music is easy—the music's all there, all the time."

John's work connects firmly with his childhood; an only child invariably creates his own surreal world and John Lennon was no exception. In his aunt's house he was often alone and spent much of his time either reading books or writing and drawing. When he was seven he started making his own series of books, filling them with jokes, cartoons, drawings, and collages. The looking-glass world of Lewis Carroll was his love and inspiration: "I was passionate about *Alice in Wonderland* and drew all the characters—I did poems in the style of Jabberwocky. I used to *live* Alice." Then his childhood dreams were taken over by a more immediate fantasy, the adolescent world of gangs and leather, cafes and jukeboxes. John's sensibilities would always be influenced by these magic images from his childhood and his Liverpudlian teddyboy habits.

The young John Lennon with his Aunt Mimi.

In the early Beatle days John's work was full of autobiographical innuendos, but only certain aspects of his personality were revealed in the symbolism that he developed. Reality floated somewhere, bound up, before long, with his psychological difficulties. For a time drugs helped to buffer these inadequacies and also reveal new horizons. Searching for meaning, for explanations, John began to use his songs more and more as an emotional release, often in the form of a confession of inner conflict. T. S. Eliot wrote that the artist's progress is a "continued extinction of personality," emphasizing the gap between "the man who suffers and the mind which creates." It is John's narrowing of this gap, to the extent that it is almost unrecognizable, which I feel has contributed to the power of his songs. For John is an artist whose ideas and attitudes only hang together in the context of his own experience.

In his songs John gives us hieroglyphic glimpses of himself, insights into the personality of a "Nowhere Man" who "doesn't have a point of view," to a "holy roller" with "hair down to his knee." He has described the pain of heroin withdrawal: "My feet are so heavy/so is my head/I wish I was a baby/I wish I was dead." John has shared his interior world with us; and though he feels that his most creative work was born out of inner pain and conflict, his inspiration has also come from happiness. "To hell with everything except the inner necessity for expression and the medium of expression," said Dylan Thomas, "everything except the great need of forever striving after this mystery and meaning I moan about." The imagery in many of John's songs derives its power from his obsessions and the energy with which he has tried to master them: "Working Class Hero," "God," "Isolation," and "Nobody Loves You (When You're Down and Out)" are a few examples. Here John exposes his neurotic disposition for all to see, his feelings of anxiety and inadequacy—and self-insulating arrogance.

"In his solitude, which is his inheritance, the modern artist has had to learn that the universe which he is going to write or paint is in *himself*. He has learned that this universe which he carried about in himself is singularly personal and unique as well as universal," wrote Wallace Fowlie in *The Age of Surrealism*. John started to realize this in 1964, when there was a transition between his poetry and his song lyrics: "I started being *me* about the songs, not writing them objectively, but subjectively . . . I started thinking about my own emotions—I don't know when exactly it started. Probably in some like "I'm a Loser" or "Hide Your Love Away."*

"Help" was John's first song about pain, about John suffocating inside his Beatle image: "And now my life has changed in oh so many ways/My

*Lennon Remembers: The Rolling Stone Interviews, Straight Arrow Books, San Francisco, 1971.

independence seems to vanish in the haze/But now and then I feel so insecure . . ." He was still unsure then about projecting his own feelings: "I always wrote about me when I could. I didn't really enjoy writing third person songs about people who lived in concrete flats and things like that. I like first person music. But because of my hang-ups, and many other things, I would only now and then specifically write about me."* After the Beatles stopped touring in 1966, creating music in a recording studio became a way of life, and since that time John has been most at home in the intimacy of a studio environment.

"I enjoy being in the studio the most, I always did," John said recently. "It's more like writing. Writing is something personal. Whether it's shyness or whatever, I never meant to be on a stage—which turned out to be great, too, for a while, but writing and recording are the best."

On his journey to self-discovery John has progressed through many changes and has been led in many wrong directions. Here was the man who had everything, adored by a vast army of youth, and yet he would "give you everything I've got for a little peace of mind." He never wanted to be a leader, although others tried to place him in that role and tried to use his name and image. I saw him talked into being the star attraction for the Toronto Peace Festival, and he was later seduced into waving the flag on behalf of Rubin and Hoffman. John had somehow felt *responsible* to produce peace, felt an *obligation* to write songs that people would sing in the pub or on demonstrations. But time and again he would come back to the philosophy that it's in your own head, the answers are within yourself.

This vulnerability to outside influences lies at the core of John's personality, and I always had trouble relating it to his aggressiveness and the power that he commanded. It seemed almost out of character for somebody as dominating as John Lennon to be so easily used and misled. Surely he would learn, I kept thinking. Then in a new situation he would be weak again, and go along with something he didn't really want to do. One day at Apple he tried to shed some light on this: "I'm inclined to go along first, and then work it out. Whatever I'm really thinking about, I don't find out till later. Because of the type of person I am I'm more likely to say 'yes, OK'—that's how I am. If you offer me this I'm inclined to say, 'OK, stick it on the wall,' yer know, 'OK, paint it green—alright, that's alright,' and only after I'll think I didn't actually want to do that. But because of the situation that person's personality overpowers mine. I'm inclined to go along with the guy—any fucker—that comes up and sort of says, 'this is how we should do it'—it takes a lot of strength on my part

John created this wall painting/collage in the middle of the night in Stephen Sanders' house, London, shortly before the release of "Sgt. Pepper" in 1967.

*Lennon Remembers: The Rolling Stone Interviews. Straight Arrow Books, San Francisco, 1971.

not to do it. And that's just how I am. I'm always bitter after the event."

This weakness was an obvious handicap, and led to his frustration within the Beatles. When his ideas were continually thwarted by Paul, who had become the dominant member of the group, John's creativity suffered and was repressed for a long period.

The period of Primal Therapy in 1970 was the dividing line in John's work. Since that time he has been involved with a new kind of creativity and exhibits what Freud has spoken of as a "lack of repression." Though there were flashes of this maturity before therapy, something new was happening in "Cold Turkey," and the period from 1968, when John first became involved with Yoko, until the beginning of therapy was a time of intense growth.

In the beginning, it seemed that Yoko liberated John through love, liberated him of false values and false roles. But he became overdependent on Yoko, the person who had given him "freedom." John felt that he could not live without her, so it was a vicarious freedom, and for a time he was living through Yoko. Invariably I saw him retreat behind her to avoid a situation he couldn't face up to. Later, he discovered through therapy that freedom must come from within and must be self-generated. Yoko's achievement was that she helped him with the first step toward becoming free, and helped him to recognize the inhibited part of himself. One of the purposes of intimate relationships is to remove the mask, to penetrate through the persona, and beyond, to find the *emotional self*—and in this sense their relationship was rewarding to John.

In 1970, John said "the dream is over. It's just the same, only I'm thirty and a lot of people have got long hair." He spoke not only for himself but for a generation. During his peace crusade, he had focused on a troubled world. His eyes were opened to the human condition, to man's inhumanity to man, and the cruelty of the system. John was a part of a general awakening, but his eloquence on behalf of peace revealed the strength of his beliefs, and the part he played was important. As Robert Kennedy said: "Each time a man stands up for an ideal, or acts to improve the lot of others, or strikes out against injustice, he sends forth a ripple of hope, and crossing each other from a million different centers of energy and daring those ripples build a current that can sweep down the mightiest wall of oppression." John's dream did not end, even though he thought it had. "Imagine" showed a renewed optimism and idealism: "You may say that I'm the dreamer,/but I'm not the only one."

Day to day living has brought a new set of complexities for John. In recent years he has created consciously or unconsciously, extraordinary situations that he would have to write about, situations that pushed him to the very edge of his lifeline. John compares this state of being to the time when he was at school: "I was always just on the verge of being kicked out of school, but I always just managed to come through somehow—so I rely on my own instincts to avoid actual falling off the cliff—I'm a survivor not a suicidal type." Part of the problem has been a revolt against growing up, against facing the fact of age. Yet John would become equally frustrated by not growing up. "I have this great fear of this *normal* thing—you know, the ones that didn't become rock and rollers, the ones that settled for it, settled for the *deal*! That's what I'm trying to avoid. But I'm sick of avoiding it with violence . . . I've gotta do it some other way."

Everything has fallen into place for John since he and Yoko were reunited, and the birth of their son has given them both a renewed vision, another reason for "faith in the future outta the now." John's lifestyle today is relaxed, without pressure: "Peace and quiet and a piano—it's basically that, and occasionally spurting out to some event, just to prove I'm still alive!"

"I do think in terms of the long term. I'm an artist. I have to express myself. I can't be dominated by gold records—the art is more important than the thing and sometimes I have to remind meself of it. Because there's a danger there, for all of us, for everyone who's involved in whatever art they're in, of *needing that love so badly* . . ."

John's alchemy is in his music—his innate ability to transpose, to be inspired both by his surroundings and by his own inner feelings, forever leading him forward to the next step on his heraldic journey. The vibrations of John Lennon have pierced our sensory rainbow in the past and surely will in the future, but above all John has given us a vision for today, as we all share in the essences of the *now*, living and cherishing life as it comes, one day at a time.

JOHN LENNON CHRONOLOGY

1940

October 9
John Winston Lennon is born in Liverpool Maternity Hospital in Liverpool, England, during an air-raid. His parents, Alfred Lennon and Julia Stanley, have been married since December 3, 1938.

1942

Fred Lennon, working as a steward, deserts his ship and loses contact with the family. John is taken in by his Aunt Mimi, Julia's sister.

1945

Fred Lennon returns to England and visits John. He takes John with him for a holiday in Blackpool, and starts to make plans for them both to emigrate to New Zealand. Julia arrives and there is a confrontation: John wants to stay with his father but at the last moment runs out of the house after his mother. She takes him back to Mimi to be brought up.

1946

John enters Dovedale Primary School, Liverpool.

1952

John enters Quarrybank School, Liverpool.

1955

John forms a skiffle group named the Quarrymen.

1956

June 15
Paul McCartney, age fourteen, is introduced to sixteen-year-old John at the Woolton Parish Church in Liverpool.

1957

John starts attending Liverpool Art College. He is put into the lettering class, which he hates. In the same class is a girl named Cynthia Powell.

1960

John forms the Beatles.

April
The group visits Hamburg, Germany, to play as the Silver Beatles.

1961

The Beatles return to play in Hamburg.

1962

January/April/May
The Beatles return to Hamburg's Star Club.

August 23
John marries Cynthia Powell at Mount Pleasant Registry Office, Liverpool.

September 4-11
The Beatles' first recording sessions at EMI Studios, St. John's Wood, London, with George Martin as producer.

1963

March 7
Beatles' album *Please, Please Me* is released in England.

1964

March 23
John Lennon in His Own Write, John's first book of prose and poetry, is published.

April 18
Julian Lennon is born at Sefton General Hospital, Liverpool.

August 19/September 21
Beatles' first tour of U.S.A. and Canada.

1965

June 24
A Spaniard in the Works, John's second book, published.

October 26
Beatles presented with M.B.E. (Member of the British Empire) medals by Her Majesty the Queen at an investiture at Buckingham Palace.

December 3
Beatles' album *Rubber Soul* released.

1966

August 5
Beatles' album *Revolver* released.

September
Yoko Ono arrives in London for the "Destruction of Art" symposium at the Institute of Contemporary Arts.

September/October
John's solo movie debut in Richard Lester's *How I Won the War* on location in Germany and Spain.

November 9-12
Yoko's exhibition of "Unfinished Paintings and Objects by Yoko Ono" at the Indica Gallery. John meets Yoko at the preview of her exhibition at the Indica Gallery in London.

1967

Yoko's "Wrapping Event" in Trafalgar Square.

June 1
Beatles' album *Sgt. Pepper's Lonely Hearts Club Band* released.

August
World premiere of Yoko Ono's *Film No. 4, (Bottoms)* at the Jacey Tattler.

August 27
Brian Epstein dies of drug overdose, London.

September
Yoko's "Half Wind Show" exhibition, presented as "Yoko Plus Me" at London's Lisson Gallery, sponsored by John Lennon.

September/November
Beatles make film *Magical Mystery Tour.*

December 7
Opening of the Beatles' Apple Shop at 94 Baker St., London.

1968

February/April
Beatles go to Rishikesh, India, for Transcendental Meditation course at the Maharishi's academy.

April
Apple Corp. Ltd. begins operating from 95 Wigmore St., London.

May
Yoko visits John for the first time at Kenwood, his country house in Weybridge, and they spend the night listening to John's experimental tapes and then make one themselves. John and Yoko's first art venture together at the Arts Lab, Drury Lane, London.

June 15
John and Yoko's "Acorn Event" at the National Sculpture Exhibition, Coventry Cathedral. John and Yoko plant acorns in the ground at the preview as a conceptual, "Living-Art," sculpture: "A symbol of East and West coming together," says John.

June 18
Opening of the National Theatre production of *In His Own Write,* adapted from John's books by Adrienne Kennedy and Victor Spinetti for the stage as a one-act play, at Old Vic Theatre, London.

July 1
John's first art exhibition "You Are Here"—a circular white canvas, assorted charities' collecting boxes, and 360 white balloons released into the sky—at Robert Frazer Gallery, Mayfair.

October 18
John and Yoko arrested by police on drugs charge. They are remanded at Marylebone Magistrate's Court, London, on bail.

November 8
Decree *nisi* granted in divorce case between John and Cynthia Lennon.

November 21
Yoko in Queen Charlotte Hospital where she suffers a miscarriage. John sleeps on the floor beside her bed. They have previously recorded the baby's heartbeat.
The Beatles' *White Album* (double album) released. John's favorite songs are: "I'm So Tired" and "Happiness is a Warm Gun." He thinks his songs on this album are the best group of songs he has ever recorded.

November 28
John fined 150 pounds with 20 guineas' cost after he has admitted possessing cannabis resin.

November 29
John and Yoko's *Two Virgins* album released.

October/November
John and Yoko's films *Smile* and *Two Virgins* premiered at Chicago Film Festival.

December 11
John and Yoko take part in the Rolling Stones' *Rock 'n' Roll Circus* filming.

December 18
John and Yoko appear at the ''Alchemical Wedding'' (the Underground's Christmas party at the Royal Albert Hall) onstage inside a large white bag.

1969

January
Beatles film and record *Let It Be* at Twickenham Studios.

January 30
Beatles record ''Get Back'' on the roof of the Apple building for the film.

February 3
Beatles appoint American businessman Allen Klein as advisor.

March 2
John and Yoko in avant-garde jazz concert at Lady Mitchell Hall, Cambridge.

March 20
John and Yoko secretly married in Gibraltar. Bed-In for peace at the Amsterdam Hilton during a week of their honeymoon. The couple talk to the world's press from their bed in the presidential suite.

March 31
Rape (Film No. 6) world premiere on Austrian National Television (73 min.) with Hans Priener as producer. John and Yoko hold a press conference in a bag at the Sacher Hotel, in Vienna, to discuss the film.

April
John and Yoko start their own office at Apple with art critic Anthony Fawcett as coordinator.

April 22
In an official ceremony performed by

the Commissioner for Oaths on the roof of Apple, John changes his middle name from Winston to Ono.

May 2
John and Yoko's album *Life With the Lions—Unfinished Music No. 2* released.

May 16
John and Yoko attempt to join Ringo, Peter Sellers, and *The Magic Christian* crew on board the QE 2 for a transatlantic crossing to stage a Bed-In in the United States. After their luggage is stowed on board, John's visa to enter the U.S. fails to come through; further plans to join the QE 2 by helicopter in mid-channel in the event of a late visa acceptance are also aborted.

May 24
In the face of the U.S. authorities' refusal to allow John into the country, the Lennons decide that the next best thing is to hold another Bed-In near enough to the American shores to broadcast their peace messages. After a false start in the Bahamas, which they found hot and inhospitable, the Lennons fly to Toronto, Canada.

May 26
John and Yoko, Derek Taylor, and film crew check into the Queen Elizabeth Hotel in Montreal and begin the Montreal Bed-In, which continues for ten days.

May 31
''Give Peace A Chance'' recorded from the Lennons' bed, with Timothy and Rosemary Leary, Tommy Smothers, Rabbi Feinberg, and the Canadian chapter of the Hare Krishnas all adding their voices.

May 30
The Beatles' single ''The Ballad of John and Yoko'' released; it chronicles John and Yoko's efforts to get married, the eventful marriage, the Bed-In and Bag event in Vienna, and is recorded by John and Paul on their own.

June 7
John and Yoko appear on ''The David Frost Show.''

June 29
John and Yoko, along with Julian (John's son) and Kyoko (Yoko's daughter) start a motoring holiday in Scotland to visit several of John's relatives.

July 1
While John is driving he loses control

of the car and it goes into a ditch. The whole family is taken to the hospital for treatment for shock and to receive stitches.

July 6
John and Yoko fly home from Scotland via a chartered plane.

July 7
''Plastic Ono Band''—in the shape of perspex robots—unveiled on the stage of the Chelsea Town Hall to promote the group's first single, ''Give Peace A Chance.''

July/August
The Beatles in the EMI Abbey Road studio to record a new album, *Abbey Road*. Yoko, whose back is sprained from the car accident, moves her bed into the studio.

August
John and Yoko buy Tittenhurst Park, Ascot—a Georgian mansion, with eighty acres of spectacularly landscaped grounds—for 150,000 pounds.
Bob Dylan, after his Isle of Wight concert, accompanies John and Yoko and George Harrison in a helicopter flight to Tittenhurst Park. John tries to get him to play piano on ''Cold Turkey,'' which he has just written, but Dylan leaves after a short stay.

September
''Two Evenings with John and Yoko,'' presented at the New Cinema Club, London, include *Two Virgins, Smile, Honeymoon,* and the world premiere of *Self-Portrait*. John and Yoko fool the critics by sending a substitute couple inside a bag, who arrive in the white Rolls to the click of the flashbulbs, walk down the aisle, and sit on the stage chanting ''Hare Krishna'' throughout the film show. John gets the audience's reaction on infra-red film.
John and Yoko and Plastic Ono Band (Eric Clapton, Klaus Voormann, and Alan White) fly to Toronto to perform live at the ''Toronto Rock 'n' Roll Revival,'' Varsity Stadium.

October
''Cold Turkey'' single released by John Lennon and Plastic Ono Band.

October 20
John and Yoko's *Wedding Album* released, a souvenir in sound and pictures of their Gibraltar wedding and subsequent Bed-In honeymoon, consisting of a boxed set of two albums, a book of press clippings, a photo of a piece of wedding cake enclosed in a plastic bag, a postcard,

and pictures of the wedding—the whole package beautifully designed by John Kosh.

November
John and Yoko on holiday in Athens, Greece.

November 26
John returns his M.B.E. medal to the Queen to protest against Britain's involvement in Biafra and support of America in Vietnam, and against ''Cold Turkey'' slipping down the charts.

November
Live Peace In Toronto album released by John and Yoko and the Plastic Ono Band.

December 15
John and Yoko and an augmented ''Plastic Ono Supergroup'' play live at the Lyceum Gallery for a UNICEF benefit.
The B.B.C. TV show ''24 Hours'' makes a one-hour documentary on John, filming him at home in Tittenhurst, driving up to London in the back of the white Rolls, in the Apple office, and on location in Sussex shooting John's film *Apotheosis*.

December 16
John and Yoko fly to Toronto, Canada, to announce the Mosport Park Peace Festival. They stay on Ronnie Hawkins' farm five days, talking to radio stations, giving peace interviews, entertaining Dick Gregory and other guests, and skidooing on the snow-covered fields.

December 17
Press conference at the Ontario Science Centre.

December 18-20
John signs his 3,000 erotic lithographs, *Bag One*, at the Hawkins' farmhouse, with help from Ed Newman and Anthony Fawcett.

December 19
John and Yoko meet Marshall McLuhan for a 45-minute television discussion, filmed by C.B.C. Television.

December 21
John and Yoko and entourage take a private train to Montreal and Ottawa. In Montreal they attend a press conference at the Chateau Champlain Hotel. In the Montreal station John and Yoko meet secretly with members of the LeDain Drug Commission.

December 22
At 11:00 A.M. John and Yoko arrive at

the Parliament buildings for a 51-minute meeting with Prime Minister Trudeau.
At the Ministry of Health John and Yoko attend an open meeting with the Health Minister, John Munro, and senior members of his department.

December 23
The Lennons return to London.

December 29
John and Yoko fly to Aalborg, Denmark, to visit Yoko's daughter, Kyoko, Yoko's first husband, Tony Cox, and his girlfriend, Melinda. They go into retreat on the farm, meditating and dieting. Hammrick and Leonard are flown in from Canada, supposedly to help John and Yoko give up smoking by hypnotism. Ritchie Yorke and John Brower arrive in Aalborg to discuss Peace Festival plans and Allen Klein arrives from New York. John and Yoko cut their hair in skinhead style.

December 31
A.T.V. Television screens *Man of the Decade,* a three-part film which looks in depth at John Lennon, John F. Kennedy, and Mao Tse-Tung, directed by Colin Clark, with commentary by Desmond Morris. The 20-minute interview with John is both entertaining and revealing.

1970

January 26
John writes, records, and mixes ''Instant Karma'' in one day, with the help of Phil Spector producing.

February
John performs on B.B.C.'s ''Top of the Pops'' to promote ''Instant Karma.''
Yoko's *Grapefruit* book published in the U.S. by Simon and Schuster.
Bag One, John's erotic lithographs show, is premiered in the U.S. at the Lee Nordness Gallery in New York and exhibited at the Denise René Gallery in Paris.
John and Yoko donate their shorn hair to Michael X's ''Blackhouse'' in North London.

March
American psychologist, Arthur Janov's book *The Primal Scream* arrives in the mail at Tittenhurst Park.
Arthur Janov flies to London to start Primal Therapy with John and Yoko.

April 10
Paul McCartney announces he has left the Beatles ''because of personal,

business and musical differences,'' and releases his solo album.

May 8
The Beatles' *Let It Be* album finally released, produced by Phil Spector.

May
Let It Be, a documentary film featuring the Beatles (88 minutes), has its world premiere.

April-August
John and Yoko are at the Primal Institute in Los Angeles, undergoing Primal Therapy. They live in a rented house in Bel-Air.
Back in Tittenhurst Park, John records his first solo album, *John Lennon/Plastic Ono Band,* in his recently completed 16-track studio.

December
John and Yoko visit New York, spend time with Jonas Mekas and make the films *Up Your Legs* and *Fly.*

December 30
Paul McCartney begins High Court proceedings to end the Beatles' partnership.

1971

January 21
John's interview with Jann Wenner published in two parts in *Rolling Stone* under the title ''The Working Class Hero.''

March 10
In the English High Court, a receiver is appointed to handle the Beatles' assets, and Allen Klein is prevented from further management of the group's affairs.

March 12
John Lennon and the Plastic Ono Band release ''Power to the People''/''Open Your Box'' single.

May 15
The Filmmakers' Fortnight Festival in Cannes, France, shows *Apotheosis* (18 minutes, directed by John Lennon) and *Fly* (directed by Yoko Ono Lennon, 50 minutes).

June 6
John and Yoko join Frank Zappa and The Mothers of Invention in concert at New York's Fillmore East.

July
John records the *Imagine* album at his studio in Tittenhurst Park, at the same

time filming every session and special sequences for the *Imagine* film.

August
John and Yoko fly to the Virgin Islands in search of Kyoko and continue on to New York.
John and Yoko decide to settle in New York, and rent an apartment in the West Village and a work loft in SoHo.

September 5
The London Art Spectrum at Alexandria Palace, London, screens five John and Yoko films: *Cold Turkey, The Ballad of John and Yoko, Give Peace a Chance, Instant Karma,* and *Up Your Legs.*

September 9
John's *Imagine* album released.

October 9-27
''This is Not Here'' exhibition by Yoko Ono with John Lennon as guest artist at the Everson Museum of Art, Syracuse, New York.

October
John and Yoko protest on behalf of the American Indian's civil rights, in Syracuse, New York.

November
John plays at the Attica benefit at the Apollo Theater in New York.

December 1
''Happy Xmas (War is Over)'' single released by John and the Yoko Ono Plastic Ono Band with the Harlem Community Choir.

December 11
John and Yoko appear at a John Sinclair benefit in Ann Arbor, Michigan.

1972

January
The staff of the Senate Internal Security Subcommittee of the Judiciary Committee prepares and submits to Senator Strom Thurmond a memo about John's radical involvements with Jerry Rubin, Abbie Hoffman, and Rennie Davis.

February 14
John and Yoko co-host ''The Mike Douglas Show'' for one week. Chuck Berry guests on one show and plays live with John.

February 29
John's U.S. non-immigrant visa expires.

February 4
Senator Strom Thurmond writes to John Mitchell, then attorney general, attaching the memo about John's radical involvements with the note: ''This appears to me to be an important matter, and I think it would be well for it to be considered at the highest level as I can see many headaches might be avoided if appropriate action be taken in time.'' Mitchell also sends a copy of the same memo to a White House aide.

March 6
The visa extension granted to John five days earlier is revoked by Sol Marks, New York INS district director.

April 29
John Lindsay, mayor of New York, asks the federal authorities to allow John and Yoko to remain permanently in America and to quash the deportation proceedings.

April 24
''Woman Is The Nigger Of The World'' single, jointly written by John and Yoko and performed by the John Lennon Plastic Ono Band with Elephant's Memory, released.
John guests on ''The Dick Cavett Show'' and says he is being followed by government agents and that his phone is tapped.

June 12
Sometime in New York City (double album) released by John and Yoko with Elephant's Memory.

August 30
''One to One'' charity concert at Madison Square Garden: John and Yoko and Elephant's Memory plus an all-star supporting bill stage two shows for the Willowbrook handicapped children's homes. The concert is simulcasted on ABC Television.
World premiere of John and Yoko's film *Erection.* The film shows a time-lapse view of a London hotel's construction, using hundreds of photographs taken from the same position over several years by Iain McMillan.

December 23
World premiere of John and Yoko's film *Imagine* on U.S. television.

1973

March
John ordered to leave the U.S. by immigration authorities.

Yoko wins custody of Kyoko, now eight years old, from ex-husband in the U.S. courts, but father Tony Cox disappears with the girl.

March-July
Ringo records John's song "I Am the Greatest" for his album Ringo, which is released November 2, 1973.

June
Allen Klein sues John for $200,000.

October
John and Yoko separate for the first time since 1968. John flies to Los Angeles to get away from the immigration problems.

October 26
"Mind Games"/"Meat City" single released by John Lennon.

November 2
Mind Games album released by John Lennon and The Plastic U.F. Ono Band.

October-December
John persuades Phil Spector to produce his rock 'n' roll oldies album and they go into the Record Plant studios in Los Angeles with an ever-changing group of thirty musicians to lay down tracks.

November
John, Paul, and George sue Allen Klein.

1974

January
John asks the Queen for a Royal Pardon in connection with his five-year-old drug conviction: "So as to be free to travel to and from the U.S."

March
John ejected from the Troubadour Club in Los Angeles after heckling the Smothers Brothers.

March-May
John produces Harry Nilsson's Pussy Cats album in Los Angeles.

July 17
John ordered by U.S. Justice Department to leave the U.S. within sixty days or be deported. John lodges an appeal.

August
With one song written, John returns to New York to work on a new album

and appear in the immigration case proceedings.
In New York's Record Plant John records all the songs for Walls and Bridges.
John helps Elton John in the recording studios, playing guitar and singing back-up vocal on Elton's version of his song "Lucy In the Sky With Diamonds," and playing guitar on Elton's version of another of John's songs "One Day At A Time." Both songs are released as a single on November 15, 1974.
Ringo records John's song "Goodnight Vienna" for his album of the same name released November 15, 1974.

August 23
John sees a U.F.O. at 9:00 from the roof of his building.

August 31
John claims in the U.S. federal court that the Nixon Administration tried to have him deported because they had heard he was one of the organizers of an antiwar demonstration due to be held at the Republican Convention in Miami in 1972.

September
The Board of Immigration Appeals orders John to leave the U.S. voluntarily by September 8 or be deported. He lodges another appeal.

September 23
"Whatever Gets You Through The Night" single by John Lennon released (with Elton John on piano and back-up vocal).

September 26
Walls and Bridges album by John Lennon with the Plastic Ono Nuclear Band released.

October 21-25
John returns to the Record Plant to record more songs for his Rock 'n' Roll album, this time producing on his own.

November 28
John joins Elton John on stage at Madison Square Garden during Elton's Thanksgiving concert. They play "Whatever Gets You Thru The Night," "Lucy In The Sky With Diamonds," and "I Saw Her Standing There."

December
Rolling Stone reveals details of the illegal conspiracy to deport John from the U.S.
John, his son Julian, and his secretary May Pang stay at Florida's Disney World over the New Year holidays.

1975

January
The Beatles' final dissolution in London.
John and Yoko are reunited and John returns to live with her at their Dakota apartment in New York.

January 2
U.S. District Court Judge Richard Owen rules in favor of John and his lawyers, permitting them access to the immigration files under certain conditions.

January
John plays on David Bowie's sessions for the Young Americans album, co-writing a song with Bowie, "Fame," and playing guitar on Bowie's version of his own song "Across The Universe." "Young Americans" is released June 2, 1975. "He's the last great original," Bowie says of Lennon.

February
Morris Levy of Adam VIII Records starts marketing Roots, an album put together from a rough tape of John's rock 'n' roll oldies.

February 15
Capitol Records rush release of the John Lennon Rock 'n' Roll album. The Roots album is stopped under threat of legal action after 3,000 copies have been sold. Levy starts a lawsuit for $42 million.

March
John and Yoko's first public appearance together after the end of their separation at the Grammy Awards presentations.

June
John files suit in Manhattan federal court against former Attorney General John Mitchell, former Attorney General Richard Kleindienst, and other government officials of INS, charging that the deportation actions directed against him are improper.

September
The Immigration and Naturalization Service grants John a temporary non-priority status because of Yoko's pregnancy.

October 7
The U.S. Court of Appeals overturns the order to deport John. John's battle with the immigration authorities is over. The Court of Appeals rules that the British law under which John has been convicted is unjust by U.S. standards, and that therefore he has been denied due process.

October 9
Sean Ono Lennon, a healthy 8-lb., 10-oz. boy, is born in New York Hospital (on John's birthday). "I feel higher than the Empire State Building," John says.

October 24
The Shaved Fish album, a collection of John's songs from 1969 to 1975, released.

1976

January-February
The lawsuit in U.S. District Court between John and Morris Levy regarding the Rock 'n' Roll album and John's earlier infringement of the copyright to Chuck Berry's "You Can't Catch Me."

February 20
Judge Griesa delivers a 29-page opinion on the Levy/Lennon suit, stating that there has been a tentative verbal agreement between Lennon and Levy but that Lennon has entered into it "not as a free agent."

March
John's countersuit against Levy is heard. Capitol, EMI, and John ask for reimbursement of their lost income; John also asks for punitive damages due to the loss of quality and possible damages to his career. Judge Griesa awards John $45,000 for damages to his reputation.

May
John and Yoko, baby Sean, and his governess fly to Los Angeles for John to hold business discussions and also to spend time with Ringo in a recording studio working on his new album.

June
John and Yoko and family move to a house on Long Island for the summer. Capitol Records repackages old Beatle material in the two-album set The Beatles, Rock 'n' Roll Music.

July 27
John's application to remain in the United States as a permanent resident is formally approved at a special hearing before Immigration Judge Ira Fieldsteel, when he is given his long-sought green card, No. A17-597-321. John says after the hearing that, "the same as everyone else," he plans to devote himself to his "wife, kids and a job."

JOHN LENNON DISCOGRAPHY

ALBUMS

1968

UNFINISHED MUSIC NO. 1: TWO VIRGINS
Prod.: John Lennon and Yoko Ono
Recorded: May 1968

Side One:
Two Virgins   John Lennon, Yoko Ono (14:02)

Two Virgins No. 1
Together
Two Virgins No. 2
Two Virgins No. 3
Two Virgins No. 4
Two Virgins No. 5
Two Virgins No. 6

Side Two:
Two Virgins   John Lennon, Yoko Ono (15:00)

Hushabye Hushabye
Two Virgins No. 7
Two Virgins No. 8
Two Virgins No. 9
Two Virgins No. 10

(US) Apple T 5001 Distributed by
 Tetragammation Records Nov. 11, 1968
(UK) Apple SAPCOR 2 Distributed by Track
 Records Nov. 29, 1968

1969

UNFINISHED MUSIC NO. 2: LIFE WITH THE LIONS
Prod.: John Lennon and Yoko Ono
Side One Recorded Live: March 2, 1969 at
 Lady Mitchell Hall, Cambridge, England
Side Two recorded: Nov. 4-25, 1968

Side One:
''Cambridge 1969''   John Lennon, Yoko Ono
 (26:30)

Song For John
Cambridge 1969
Let's Go On Flying
Snow Is Falling All The Time
Mummy's Only Looking For Her Hand In The
 Snow

Side Two:
No Bed For Beatle   Lennon, Yoko Ono 4:45
Baby's Heartbeat   Lennon, Yoko Ono 5:10
Two Minutes Silence   Lennon, Yoko Ono 2:00
Radio Play   Lennon, Yoko Ono 12:35

(UK) Zapple 01 May 9, 1969
(US) Zapple ST 3357 May 26, 1969

WEDDING ALBUM
Prod.: John Lennon and Yoko Ono
Recorded: March-April 1969

Side One:
John and Yoko   Lennon, Yoko Ono (22:23)

Side Two:
Amsterdam   Lennon, Yoko Ono (24:52)

(US) Apple SMAX 3361 Oct. 20, 1969
(UK) Apple SAPCOR 11 Nov. 7, 1969

THE PLASTIC ONO BAND—LIVE PEACE IN TORONTO 1969
Prod.: John Lennon and Yoko Ono
Recorded Live: Sept. 13, 1969 at the Toronto
 Rock 'n' Roll Revival, Varsity Stadium,
 Toronto, Canada

Side One:
Introduction of the Band 1:44
Blue Suede Shoes   Carl Perkins 2:09
Money (That's What I Want)   Berry Gordy,
 Janie Bradford 3:20
Dizzy Miss Lizzie   Larry Williams 3:25
Yer Blues   Lennon/McCartney 3:50
Cold Turkey   Lennon 3:43
Give Peace A Chance   Lennon 3:30

Side Two:
Don't Worry Kyoko (Mummy's Only Looking
 For Her Hand In The Snow)   Yoko Ono 4:44
John, John (Let's Hope For Peace)   Yoko
 Ono 12:54

(UK) Apple CORE 2001 Dec. 12, 1969
(US) Apple SW 3362 Dec. 12, 1969

1970

JOHN LENNON/PLASTIC ONO BAND
Prod.: John Lennon, Yoko Ono, Phil Spector
Recorded: October 1970

Side One:
Mother   Lennon 5:29
Hold On (John)   Lennon 1:49
I Found Out   Lennon 3:33
Working Class Hero   Lennon 3:44
Isolation   Lennon 2:48

Side Two:
Remember   Lennon 4:29
Love   Lennon 3:17
Well Well Well   Lennon 5:52
Look At Me   Lennon 2:49
God   Lennon 4:04
My Mummy's Dead   Lennon 0:48

(UK) Apple PCS 7124 Dec. 11, 1970
(US) Apple SW 3372 Dec. 11, 1970

YOKO ONO/PLASTIC ONO BAND
Prod.: John Lennon and Yoko Ono
Recorded: October 1970, February 1968 °

Side One:
Why   Yoko Ono 5:30
Why Not   Yoko Ono 10:39
Greenfield Morning I Pushed An Empty Baby
 Carriage All Over The City   Yoko Ono 5:40

Side Two:
°AOS   Yoko Ono 7:06
Touch Me   Yoko Ono 3:40
Paper Shoes   Yoko Ono 8:10

(UK) Apple SAPCOR 17 Dec. 11, 1970
(US) Apple SW 3373 Dec. 11, 1970

1971

IMAGINE by John Lennon Plastic Ono Band
 with the Flux Fiddlers

Prod.: John Lennon, Yoko Ono, Phil Spector
Recorded: July 1971

Side One:
Imagine   Lennon 2:59
Crippled Inside   Lennon 3:43
Jealous Guy   Lennon 4:10
It's So Hard   Lennon 2:22
I Don't Want To Be A Soldier Mama, I Don't
 Want To Die   Lennon 6:01

Side Two:
Give Me Some Truth   Lennon 3:11
Oh My Love   Lennon/Yoko Ono 2:40
How Do You Sleep?   Lennon 5:29
How?   Lennon 3:37
Oh Yoko!   Lennon 4:18

(US) Apple SW 3379 Sept. 9, 1971
(UK) Apple PAS 10004 Oct. 8, 1971

FLY by Yoko Ono Plastic Ono Band with
 Joe Jones Tone Deaf Music Co.
Prod.: John Lennon and Yoko Ono
New Songs Recorded: August 1971

Side One:
Midsummer New York   Yoko Ono 3:50
Mind Train   Yoko Ono 16:52

Side Two:
Mind Holes   Yoko Ono 2:45
Don't Worry Kyoko   Yoko Ono 4:52
Mrs. Lennon   Yoko Ono 4:10
Hirake (previously Open Your Box)   Yoko Ono
 3:23
Toilet Piece/Unknown   Yoko Ono 0:30
O' Wind (Body Is The Scar Of Your
 Mind)   Yoko Ono 5:22

Side Three:
Airmale (Tone Deaf Jam)   Yoko Ono 10:40
Don't Count The Waves   Yoko Ono 5:26
You   Yoko Ono 9:00

Side Four:
Fly   Yoko Ono 22:53
Telephone Piece   Yoko Ono 1:01

(US) Apple SVBB 3380 (Double Album) Sept.
 20, 1971
(UK) Apple SAPTU 101/2 (Double Album)
 Dec. 3, 1971

1972

SOMETIME IN NEW YORK CITY by
 John Lennon and Yoko Ono
Plastic Ono Band with Elephant's Memory and
 The Invisible Strings (sides one and two)
John Lennon and Yoko Ono with The Plastic
 Ono Supergroup (side three)
John Lennon and Yoko Ono Plastic Ono Band
 with Frank Zappa and The Mothers Of
 Invention (side four)
Prod.: John Lennon, Yoko Ono, Phil Spector
Sides one and two recorded: March 1-20,
 1972
Side three recorded live: Dec. 15, 1969 at the
 Lyceum Ballroom, London
Side four recorded live: June 6, 1971 at
 Fillmore East, New York

Side One:
Woman Is The Nigger Of The World   Lennon/

Yoko Ono 5:15
Sisters, O Sisters   Yoko Ono 3:46
Attica State   Lennon/Yoko Ono 2:52
Born In A Prison   Yoko Ono 4:04
New York City   Lennon 4:32

Side Two:
Sunday Bloody Sunday   Lennon/Yoko Ono
   5:00
The Luck Of The Irish   Lennon/Yoko Ono
   2:54
John Sinclair   Lennon 3:28
Angela   Lennon/Yoko Ono 4:08
We're All Water   Yoko Ono 7:15

Record Two: Live Jam

Side Three:
Cold Turkey   Lennon 7:34
Don't Worry Kyoko   Yoko Ono 17:12

Side Four:
Well . . . (Baby Please Don't Go)   Walter Ward
   4:50
Jamrag   Lennon/Yoko Ono 1:50
Scumbag   Lennon/Yoko Ono/Frank Zappa
   12:53
Au   Lennon/Yoko Ono 3:25

(US) Apple SVBB 3392 (Double Album) June
   12, 1972
(UK) Apple PCSP 716 (Double Album)
   September 15, 1972

1973

APPROXIMATELY INFINITE UNIVERSE
by Yoko Ono Plastic Ono Band with Elephant's
   Memory, The Endless Strings and Choir Boys
Prod.: John Lennon and Yoko Ono
Recorded: October-November 1972

Side One:
Yang Yang   Yoko Ono 3:52
Death of Samantha   Yoko Ono 6:23
I Want My Love To Rest Tonight   Yoko Ono
   5:11
What Did I Do!   Yoko Ono 4:11
Have You Seen A Horizon Lately   Yoko Ono
   1.55

Side Two:
Approximately Infinite Universe   Yoko Ono
   3:19
Peter The Dealer   Yoko Ono 4:43
Song For John   Yoko Ono 2:02
Catman (The Rosies Are Coming)   Yoko Ono
   5:29
What A Bastard The World Is   Yoko Ono 4:33
Waiting For The Sunrise   Yoko Ono 2:32

Side Three:
I Felt Like Smashing My Face In A Clear Glass
   Window   Yoko Ono 5:07
Winter Song   Yoko Ono 3:37
Kite Song   Yoko Ono 3:19
What A Mess   Yoko Ono 2:41
Shirankatta (I Didn't Know)   Yoko Ono 3:13
Air Talk   Yoko Ono 3:21

Side Four:
I Have A Woman Inside My Soul   Yoko Ono
   5:31
Move On Fast   Yoko Ono 3:40
Now Or Never   Yoko Ono 4:57

Is Winter Here To Stay?   Yoko Ono 4:27
Looking Over From My Hotel Window
   Yoko Ono 3:30

(US) Apple SVBB 3399 (Double Album) Jan. 8,
   1973
(UK) Apple SAPDO 1001 (Double Album) Feb.
   16, 1973

MIND GAMES by John Lennon and The
   Plastic U.F. Ono Band
Prod.: John Lennon
Recorded: September 1973

Side One:
Mind Games   Lennon 4:10
Tight A$ Lennon 3:35
Aisumasen (I'm Sorry)   Lennon 4:41
One Day (At A Time)   Lennon 3:27
Bring On The Lucie (Freda People)   Lennon
   4:11
Nutopian International Anthem   Lennon 0:03

Side Two:
Intuition   Lennon 3:05
Out The Blue   Lennon 3:19
Only People   Lennon 3:21
I Know (I Know)   Lennon 3:56
You Are Here   Lennon 4:06
Meat City   Lennon 2:52

(US) Apple SW 3414 Nov. 2, 1973
(UK) Apple PCS 7165 Nov. 16, 1973

1974

WALLS AND BRIDGES by John Lennon with
   The Plastic Ono Nuclear Band
Prod.: John Lennon
Recorded: August 1974

Side One:
Going Down On Love   Lennon 3:53
Whatever Gets You Thru The Night   Lennon
   3:24
Old Dirt Road   Lennon/Harry Nilsson 4:10
What You Got   Lennon 4:39
Bless You   Lennon 4:39
Scared   Lennon 4:37

Side Two:
No. 9 Dream   Lennon 4:44
Surprise, Surprise (Sweet Bird Of
   Paradox)   Lennon 2:33
Steel And Glass   Lennon 4:35
Beef Jerky   Lennon 3:25
Nobody Loves You (When You're Down And
   Out)   Lennon 5:07
YaYa   Morgan Robinson/Clarence Lewis/
   Lee Dorsey 1:08

(US) Apple SW 3416 Sept. 26, 1974
(UK) Apple PCTC 253 Oct. 4, 1974

1975

ROCK 'N' ROLL by John Lennon
Prod.: John Lennon, Phil Spector*
Recorded: October 21-25, 1974; October-
   December 1973*

Side One:
Be-Bop-A-Lula   Gene Vincent/Tex Doris 2:36

Stand By Me   Ben E. King/Jerry Leiber/
   Mike Stoller 3:29
Medley: Rip It Up   Robert Blackwell/
   John Marascalco 1:06
Medley: Ready Teddy   Robert Blackwell/
   John Marascalco 0:33
*You Can't Catch Me   Chuck Berry 4:51
Ain't That A Shame   Antoine Domino/
   Dave Bartholomew
Do You Want To Dance   Bobby Freeman 2:53
*Sweet Little Sixteen   Chuck Berry 3:00

Side Two:
Slippin' And Slidin'   Richard Penniman/
   Edwin J. Bocage/Albert Collins/
   James Smith 2:16
Peggy Sue   Jerry Allison/Norman Petty/
   Buddy Holly 2:02
Medley: Bring It On Home To Me   Sam Cooke
   2:03
Medley: Send Me Some Lovin'   Lloyd Price/
   John Marascalco 1:37
*Bony Moronie   Larry Williams 3:50
YaYa   Morgan Robinson/Clarence Lewis/
   Lee Dorsey 2:17
Just Because   Lloyd Price 4:25

(US) Apple SK 3419 Feb. 17, 1975
(UK) Apple PCS 7169 Feb. 21, 1975

SHAVED FISH
Prod.: John Lennon, Yoko Ono, Phil Spector;
   John Lennon,* John Lennon and
   Yoko Ono;** Phil Spector***

Side One:
**Give Peace A Chance   Lennon/McCartney
   0:59
Cold Turkey   Lennon 4:59
***Instant Karma! (We All Shine On)   Lennon
   3:12
Power To The People   Lennon 3:04
Mother   Lennon 5:03
Woman Is The Nigger Of The World   Lennon/
   Yoko Ono 4:37

Side Two:
Imagine   Lennon 2:59
*Whatever Gets You Thru The Night   Lennon
   3:04
*Mind Games   Lennon 4:10
*No. 9 Dream   Lennon 4:44
Medley: Happy Xmas (War Is Over)   Lennon/
   Yoko Ono 3:25
Medley: *Give Peace A Chance   Lennon/
   McCartney 0:50

(US) Apple SW 3421 Oct. 24, 1975
(UK) Apple PCS 7173 Oct. 24, 1975

SINGLES

1969

A: GIVE PEACE A CHANCE   Lennon/
   McCartney 4:49
B: REMEMBER LOVE   Yoko Ono 4:01
by Plastic Ono Band
Prod.: John Lennon and Yoko Ono
A Side Recorded: June 1, 1969 in Montreal,
   Canada

(UK) Apple 13 July 4, 1969
(US) Apple 1809 July 7, 1969

A: COLD TURKEY Lennon 4:59
B: DON'T WORRY KYOKO (MUMMY'S ONLY LOOKING FOR A HAND IN THE SNOW) Yoko Ono 4:52
by Plastic Ono Band
Prod.: John Lennon and Yoko Ono
A Side Recorded: September 30, 1969

(US) Apple 1813 Oct. 20, 1969
(UK) Apple 1001 Oct. 24, 1969

1970

A: INSTANT KARMA! (WE ALL SHINE ON) Lennon 3:18
B: WHO HAS SEEN THE WIND? Yoko Ono 2:02
by John Ono Lennon with The Plastic Ono Band; Yoko Ono Lennon with The Plastic Ono Band
Prod.: Phil Spector (A side); John Lennon (B side)
A Side Recorded: January 26, 1970

(UK) Apple 1003 Feb. 6, 1970
(US) Apple 1818 Feb. 20, 1970

A: MOTHER Lennon 3:55
B: WHY Yoko Ono 5:30
by John Lennon Plastic Ono Band; Yoko Ono Plastic Ono Band
Prod.: John Lennon, Yoko Ono, Phil Spector (A side); John Lennon and Yoko Ono (B side)

(US) Apple 1827 Dec. 28, 1970

1971

A: POWER TO THE PEOPLE Lennon 3:15
B: OPEN YOUR BOX (later called **HIRAKE**) Yoko Ono 3:23
by John Lennon Plastic Ono Band; Yoko Ono Plastic Ono Band
Prod.: John Lennon, Yoko Ono, Phil Spector (A side); John Lennon and Yoko Ono (B side)
A Side Recorded: February 1971; B side recorded: February 1971; vocals recorded: March, 1971.

(UK) Apple R 5892 March 12, 1971

A: POWER TO THE PEOPLE Lennon 3:15
B: TOUCH ME Yoko Ono 3:40
by John Lennon Plastic Ono Band; Yoko Ono Plastic Ono Band
Prod.: John Lennon, Yoko Ono and Phil Spector (A side); John Lennon and Yoko Ono (B side)

(US) Apple 1830 March 22, 1971

A: MRS. LENNON Yoko Ono 4:10
B: MIDSUMMER NEW YORK Yoko Ono 3:50
by Yoko Ono Plastic Ono Band
Prod.: John Lennon and Yoko Ono

(US) Apple 1839 Sept. 29, 1971
(UK) Apple 38 Oct. 29, 1971

A: IMAGINE Lennon 2:59
B: IT'S SO HARD Lennon 2:22
by John Lennon Plastic Ono Band
Prod.: John Lennon, Yoko Ono, Phil Spector

(US) Apple 1840 Oct. 11, 1971

A: HAPPY XMAS (WAR IS OVER) Lennon/Yoko Ono 3:25
B: LISTEN, THE SNOW IS FALLING Yoko Ono 3:10
by John Lennon and Yoko Ono Plastic Ono Band with The Harlem Community Choir (A side); Yoko Plastic Ono Band (B side)
Prod.: John Lennon, Yoko Ono, Phil Spector
Recorded: Early Nov. 1971

(US) Apple 1842 Dec. 1, 1971
(UK) Apple R 5970 Nov. 24, 1972

1972

A: MIND TRAIN Yoko Ono
B: LISTEN, THE SNOW IS FALLING Yoko Ono 3:10
by Yoko Ono Plastic Ono Band
Prod.: John Lennon and Yoko Ono (A side); John Lennon, Yoko Ono, Phil Spector (B side)

(UK) Apple 41 Jan. 21, 1972

A: WOMAN IS THE NIGGER OF THE WORLD Lennon/Yoko Ono 5:15
B: SISTERS, O SISTERS Yoko Ono 3:46
by John Lennon Plastic Ono Band with Elephant's Memory and The Invisible Strings (A side); Yoko Ono Plastic Ono Band with Elephant's Memory and The Invisible Strings (B side)
Prod.: John Lennon, Yoko Ono, Phil Spector
Recorded: March, 1972

(US) Apple 1848 April 24, 1972

A: NOW OR NEVER Yoko Ono 4:57
B: MOVE ON FAST Yoko Ono 3:40
by Yoko Ono Plastic Ono Band (A side); Yoko Ono Plastic Ono Band with Elephant's Memory (B side)
Prod.: John Lennon and Yoko Ono

(US) Apple 1853 Nov. 13, 1972

1973

A: DEATH OF SAMANTHA Yoko Ono 3:40
B: YANG YANG Yoko Ono 3:52
by Yoko Ono Plastic Ono Band with Elephant's Memory, The Endless Strings and Choir Boys
Prod.: John Lennon and Yoko Ono

(US) Apple 1859 Feb. 26, 1973
(UK) Apple 47 May 4, 1973

A: WOMAN POWER Yoko Ono 4:50
B: MEN, MEN, MEN Yoko Ono 4:01
by Yoko Ono with John Lennon, guitar (A side); John Lennon, response vocal (B side)
Prod.: Yoko Ono

(US) Apple 1867 Sept. 24, 1973

A: MIND GAMES Lennon 4:10
B: MEAT CITY Lennon 2:52
by John Lennon
Prod.: John Lennon

(US) Apple 1868 Oct. 26, 1973
(UK) Apple R 5994 Nov. 16, 1973

A: (RUN, RUN, RUN)
B: MEN, MEN, MEN 4:01
by Yoko Ono with John Lennon, response vocal (B side)
Prod.: Yoko Ono

(UK) Apple 48 Nov. 9, 1973

1974

A: WHATEVER GETS YOU THRU THE NIGHT Lennon 3:24
B: BEEF JERKY Lennon 3:25
by John Lennon with The Plastic Ono Nuclear Band
Prod: John Lennon

(US) Apple 1874 Sept. 23, 1974
(UK) Apple R 5998 Oct. 4, 1974

A: NO. 9 DREAM Lennon 4:44
B: WHAT YOU GOT Lennon 3:06
by John Lennon
Prod.: John Lennon

(US) Apple 1878 Dec. 16, 1974
(UK) Apple R 6003 Jan. 31, 1975

1975

A: STAND BY ME Ben E. King/Jerry Leiber/Mike Stoller 3:29
B: MOVE OVER MRS. L. Lennon 2:56
by John Lennon
Prod.: John Lennon

(US) Apple 1881 March 10, 1975
(UK) Apple R 6005 April 18, 1975

A: IMAGINE Lennon 2:59
B: WORKING CLASS HERO Lennon 3:44
by John Lennon
Prod: John Lennon, Yoko Ono and Phil Spector

(UK) Apple R 6009 Oct. 24, 1975

JOHN LENNON SELECTED BIBLIOGRAPHY

In His Own Write, by John Lennon (Jonathan Cape, London, 1964)

A Cellarful of Noise, by Brian Epstein (Doubleday, New York, 1964)

A Spaniard in the Works, by John Lennon (Jonathan Cape, London, 1965)

Acorn Event catalog:"'Yoko' by John Lennon, 'John' by Yoko Ono" (National Sculpture Exhibition, Coventry Cathedral, May 1968)

The Beatles—The Authorized Biography, by Hunter Davies (McGraw Hill, New York, 1968)

The Beatles Illustrated Lyrics and *The Beatles Illustrated Lyrics 2,* edited by Alan Aldridge (Macdonald, London, 1969 and 1970)

Get Back, by Jonathan Cott and David Dalton (Apple, London, 1970)

Grapefruit by Yoko Ono (Simon and Schuster, New York, 1970)

Lennon Remembers: The Rolling Stone Interviews, by Jann Wenner (Straight Arrow Books, San Francisco, 1971)

Apple To The Core: The Unmaking of the Beatles, by Peter McCabe and Robert D. Schonfeld (Pocket Books, New York, 1972)

The Longest Cocktail Party, by Richard Dilello (Playboy Books, Chicago, 1972)

This Is Not Here, catalog of Yoko Ono exhibition with John Lennon guest artist (Everson Museum of Art, Syracuse, N.Y., October 1972)

As Time Goes By, by Derek Taylor (Straight Arrow Books, San Francisco, 1973)

Twilight of the Gods—The Music of the Beatles, by Wilfred Mellers (Viking Press, New York, 1973)

The Beatles: An Illustrated Record, by Roy Carr and Tony Tyler (Harmony Books, New York, 1975)

The Man Who Sold the Beatles, by Allan Williams and William Marshall (Macmillan, New York, 1975)

All Together Now: A Beatle Discography 1961—1975, by Harry Castleman and Walter Podrazik (Pierian Press, Ann Arbor, 1976)

Periodicals

"The John Lennon Interview," by Jonathan Cott, *Rolling Stone,* October 1968.

"Lennon/Ono Inc," by Betty Rolin, *Look* magazine, March 18, 1969.

"Woman Is the Nigger of the World—John and Yoko," *Nova Magazine,* March 1969.

"Bedding In For Peace: John and Yoko in Canada," by Ritchie Yorke, *Rolling Stone,* June 28, 1969.

"The Beatles: 'You Never Give Me Your Money,'" *Rolling Stone,* November 15, 1969.

"John and Yoko," by Richard Williams, *Melody Maker,* December 1969 (in two parts).

"Wedded Bliss: A Portfolio of Erotic Lithographs by John Lennon," *Avant Garde,* March 1970.

"John Rennon's Excrusive Gloupie," by Charles McCarry, *Esquire,* December 1970.

"I Wanna Hold Your Head: John Lennon After the Fall," by Andrew Kopkind, *Ramparts,* 1971.

"Yoko Ono—The Sounds Talk-In," by Steve Peacock, *Sounds,* February 20, 1971.

"Yoko Ono and Her Sixteen-Track Voice," by Jonathan Cott, *Rolling Stone,* March 18, 1971.

"Lennon: The Working-Class Hero Turns Red," by Robin Blackburn and Tariq Al, *Ramparts,* 1972.

"Lennon Plays It As It Lays—Sometime in L.A.," by Patrick Snyder-Scumpy, *Crawdaddy,* March 1974.

"Justice for a Beatle: The Illegal Plot to Prosecute and Oust John Lennon," by Joe Treen, *Rolling Stone,* December 5, 1974.

"John Lennon: His Thoughts about Music, Money, Marriage and Fame," by Lorraine Alterman, *Viva,* March 1975.

"Long Night's Journey into Day: A Conversation with John Lennon," by Pete Hamill, *Rolling Stone,* June 5, 1975.

Anthony Fawcett was born in Hillingdon Heath, England, in 1948. He was educated at Abingdon School, Berkshire, and studied Fine Art at the Ruskin School of Drawing and of Fine Art, Oxford University. He started writing regularly for *Isis*, Oxford University's weekly magazine, as art critic and art editor, and worked briefly as public relations officer for the Museum of Modern Art in Oxford.

As an art critic, he wrote a regular column for *Art and Artists* magazine and contributed to *Sculpture International*, *Studio International*, *Vogue*, and *Opus International*. In 1968, he was elected to the Association Internationale de Critiques d'Art (A.I.C.A.), and was appointed to the Organizing Committee of the National Sculpture Exhibition, Coventry Cathedral. After spending two years (1968-70) working and traveling with the Lennons, he directed the London-based company A.P.T. Enterprises (Art and Pop on Television), and traveled extensively in the United States, based for two years in California. He now lives in New York City with photographer Christina Birrer and four-year-old daughter Kristen-Eve.

David Gahr
Wisconsin-born photographer David Gahr has always worked in music, inbetween a stint of thirteen years at *Time* magazine. His preferred area of work has been with the blues men and women of our time. Gahr's photographs have been purchased by the Metropolitan Museum of Art and the Museum of Modern Art in New York. On working with Lennon, Gahr said: "I felt the same excitement in photographing John Lennon as in photographing Big Mama Thornton, Lightnin' Hopkins and Skip James—no more need be said." Photo: page 160.

Bob Gruen
Bob Gruen has been taking photos since he was eight years old and selling them since he was eleven. However, he started thinking about photography seriously when he was twenty, working mainly with rock musicians; he had been involved with rock 'n' roll from the early "Rock Around The Clock" days. Gruen's first photos of John were taken at the Attica benefit at the Apollo Theater, New York, in 1972. He met John soon after that and they have worked together on many photographic sessions and video projects since then. Gruen said of John: "He's a master of the media and the smartest person I know—I learn something every time I talk to him. He's perfect to work with. He asks what the photo is for and instinctively knows just what to do." Photos: cover photo, pages 10, 114, 122, 131(T), 133, 136, 147, 156, 174, 180, 182.

Brian Hamill
Brian Hamill spent his first fifteen years as an athlete and hanging out in Brooklyn gangs. He first started taking photos when he was sixteen—with shots of all the different kids in the gang. He studied photography for two years at the Rochester Institute of Technology. Hamill now works as a freelance photographer and recently photographed all the pictures for a book on Northern Ireland. Much of his time is spent shooting stills on movie sets, and to this date he has worked on more than twenty films. Most recently, he has been working on a new Woody Allen movie and a television play based on the early years of John F. Kennedy. Hamill found Lennon an "articulate, well-rounded artist, who really cares about his work." The last photo session he and Lennon did together was in John's New York apartment: "John had just gotten back with Yoko and he was very happy. He had given up drinking, which he was proud of, and he was into Black disco music. He loved doing photos up on the roof

and he understood exactly what I wanted—he's a totally unpretentious person." Photos: pages 26, 116, 118, 127, 128, 129, 138, 139, 140, 141, 142, 143.

Annie Leibovitz
Annie Leibovitz has been a rock 'n' roll photographer since she started in the business after studying photography at San Francisco's Art Institute in 1969. Her first photos were of Grace Slick, but her first major photographic statement was her series of Lennon portraits for *Rolling Stone*. This was an important event for her. "It was the first time I had met a legend and it was at the beginning of my career. John was a real person and he seemed to make an effort at being a human, totally in control of the situation. Working with him broke all my fears and barriers, and he was a precedent for how I have interpreted people since." Photos: page 106,110,111.

Keith McMillan
Keith McMillan is an English photographer and a former dancer with the Royal Ballet. He works in London with many leading magazines and advertising companies, including the Sunday *Times*, *Radio Times*, *Vogue*, and *Campaign*. Looking back on taking photos of John and Yoko's Acorn Event, McMillan said: "When I took these pictures I was just starting as a photographer and I found John and Yoko very cooperative—but they always did help 'new' people." Photos: pages 14, 16, 20, 22, 23, 24, 36(C), 37.

David Nutter
David Nutter is an English photographer who has been taking photos since he was sixteen. His first big job was John and Yoko's wedding. "I got this James Bond-type phone call asking me to pack my bags and camera and catch the first plane to Gibraltar. No names were given and I had to try and guess who it was. I had one camera and one lens and when I found out it was for John I was nervous as hell." Nutter went on to do many photographic sessions with John and Yoko, often at Apple. He said that John was "very patient and always trying to do something different." Nutter is still surrounded by "mad rock superstars," as he calls them, and is currently traveling with Elton John. Photos: title page, pages 43, 46, 47, 48, 72, 74, 75, 78, 80.

Chuck Pulin
After working in radio and broadcasting, Chuck Pulin got into serious photography because of the music that was happening in the middle sixties. He started covering the concerts at the

Fillmore East and this evolved into his becoming a rock photo journalist. "If I can capture on film what is going on in music and bring it to a larger audience, that's great," he explained. Pulin felt it was important to cover Lennon, and in working with him he felt John's "incredible crazy energy and zaniness." He now works out of New York City and contributes regularly to the English newspaper *Sounds*, and also to *Newsweek*, *Rolling Stone*, *Creem*, and many other publications. Photos: 120(B), 144, 145.

Ethan Russell
Ethan Russell is an American photographer who found himself in London with his first camera in 1968. Virtually the first professional shooting he did was of the Beatles in the Twickenham Studios, when they were filming and rehearsing what was later to become "Let It Be." Russell went on to work with many other rock 'n' roll groups, including the Stones and the Who. He did several sessions with John and Yoko and the resulting photos always had an edge of surreality. Russell now lives in Los Angeles, shooting, among other things, myriads of album covers. Photos: pages 32, 35, 41(B), 42, 90, 93, 94, 96, 157.

Anne Yorke
Anne Yorke is an Australian photographer/writer now living in Toronto, Canada. Her background is in advertising, and she has worked as a photo journalist team with Canadian rock writer Ritchie Yorke. She spent much time with the Lennons covering all of their Canadian peace ventures. Yorke recalled: "John was a very magical person for me—he really radiated energy and power, but on the other hand he was ordinary, just wanting his cup of tea like anybody else. John and Yoko were inseparable, mirror images in their moods and each others' alter ego." Photos: pages 31, 52, 53, 55, 60(except TL), 61, 62, 63, 64, 66, 67, 68, 76, 102, 158, 172(T).

Other Credits
Apple/EMI/Capitol Records, pages 84, 112; Robert Agriopoulos, pages 120 (T), 155; Wide World, page 36 (UL), 56, 162; Christina Birrer, pages 148, 164; Cinnemon Press, New York, pages 103, 165, 166, 168, 170, 173; Jerry Hopkins, page 60(TL); Indica Gallery, pages 28, 29, John Kelly, page 40; Cyril Maitland, *Los Angeles Magazine*, page 132; Stephen Sanders, page 178; UPI, page 38; Jurgen Vollmer (courtesy of Apple Records), page 8; Susan Wood, page 30; Tom Zimberoff, page 134.